Published by:

Lifestyle Management UK Ltd
Unit 2b Stoney House
26-30 Stoney Street
The Lace Market
Nottingham NG1 1LL
Tel +44 0115 9410 889
Fax +44 0115 9506075

Editorial:

Editor:	Rachel Blackwell
Deputy Editor:	Rosa Crisafi
Researchers:	Gemma Eason
	Rachel Blackwell
	Rosa Crisafi
	Don Bond

Design:

Art Director:	Lisa Gapp
Artists:	Lara and Max Singh

Sections in this guide were written by:

Jackie Wilson, Diane Brooks, Dr Robin Barlow, Isobelle Parr, The Iona School, Stuart Thexton, Dr Carolyn Eddleston, Karen Harvey, Pro-Tint, Gaynor Prior, Pat Hughes, Imogen Hemmingway, Tumble Tots UK Ltd, Louise Farrell, Katherine Spillar, Diane Walters, Christine Lean, Simon Eckersley, Alan Polleti & Suzanne Rudd.

Thanks to:

Simon Eckersley, my beautiful husband! Lisa Gapp for putting this whole book together, Mat Gapp, Kathryn Clifford, Sharon Burney, and all the gang at FHP magazine. Lara and Max Singh and all the lovely people that Lifestyle Management UK Ltd have met during the publication of the Absolute Guide to Parenting!

Models name: Annabelle Dixon from Grantham

Cover photography: Venture Lifestyle Photography, Nottingham

Printed and bound by: Taylor Made Print Limited

Lifestyle Management UK Ltd are required to inform you that we hold information about companies listed in the directory. Data Protection Register Number: PZ 8662731. ISBN: 0-9549221-0-7

Anti-Bullying Campaign
Tel: 020 7378 1446

Association for Postnatal Illness
Web: www.apni.org
Tel: 020 7386 0868

Baby Milk Action
Web: www.babymilkaction.org
Tel: 01223 464420

Birth Crisis Network
Tel: 01865 300266

British Allergy Foundation
Web: www.allergyfoundation.com
Tel: 020 8303 8583

British Association for Early Childhood Education
Web: www.early-education .org.uk
Tel: 020 7539 5400

British Dyslexia Association
Tel: 0118 966 8271

British Epilepsy Association
Web: www.epilepsy.org.uk
Tel: 0113 210 8800

British Institute for Brain Injured Children
Web: www.bibic.org.uk
Tel: 01278 684060

British Institute for Learning Disabilities
Web: www.bild.org.uk
Tel: 01562 723010

Cerebral Palsy Helpline (SCOPE)
Web: www.scope.org.uk
Tel: 0808 800 3333

Child Death Helpline
Tel: 0800 282 986

Children's Information Service
Web: www.childcarelink.gov.uk
Tel: 0800 960296

Cleft Lip and Palate Association (CLAPA)
Tel: 020 7431 0033

Cot Death Helpline
Tel: 0845 601 0234

Council for Disabled Children
Web: www.ncb.org.uk
Tel: 020 7843 6000

CRUSE Bereavement Care
Tel: 020 8940 4818

Down's Syndrome Association
Web: www.dsa.uk.com
Tel: 020 8682 4001

Dyspraxia Foundation
Web: www.dyspraxiafondation.org.uk
Tel: 01462 454986

Hyperactive Children's Support Group
Web: www.hacsg.org.uk
Tel: 01903 725182

Meningitis Trust
Tel: 0845 600 0800

Miscarriage Association
Web: www.miscarriageassociation.org.uk
Tel: 01924 200799

Multiple Births Foundation
Web: www.multiplebirths.org.uk
Tel: 020 8383 3519

National Asthma Campaign
Web: www.asthma.org.uk
Tel: 020 7226 2260

National Autisic Society
Web: www.nas.org.uk
Tel: 020 7833 2299

National Council for One-Parent Families
Tel: 0800 185026

National Deaf Children's Society
Tel: 020 7250 0123

National Endometriosis Society
Web: www.endo.org.uk
Tel: 020 7222 2781

NSPCC Child Protection
Tel: 0800 80 500

Parents At Work
Web: www.parentsatwork.org.uk
Tel: 020 7628 2128

Stillbirth and National Death
Web: www.uk-sands.org
Tel: 020 7436 7940

Sure Start Unit
Tel: 0115 9712631

Tax Credits
Tel: 0800 500 222

Welcome to the first edition of "The Absolute Guide to Parenting" – a comprehensive and unique A to Z directory of everything today's busy parent could need. With listings as diverse as acupuncture to local Zoo's, Yoga for children to Bookshops, our aim is to provide an all-inclusive index of services for everyone.

The Absolute Guide to Parenting is specifically tailored to expectant parents and those with young children. With our busy schedules, we don't have time to search endlessly for someone to baby-sit, a children's entertainer or a child friendly restaurant. Well, now you don't have to. With an easy referencing system – it's all at your fingertips! Need a nursery? Turn to the section and make an informed choice. With thousands of entries and hundreds of categories, you're only limited by your imagination.

Lifestyle Management UK Limited have spent the last twelve months painstakingly researching and developing the Absolute Guide so it's assessable, informative and simple to use. It's been hard work but we're sure you will love the results as much as we've loved doing it. We know your kids will too!

Finally, proceeds from this edition will be donated to the fetal care unit at the Nottingham City Hospital and the neo-natal wards at the Leicester and Derby Royal Infirmarys.

Rachel Blackwell
Editor

A1 Artists
NOTTINGHAM
Tel: 0115 9705345

Activity Island Ltd
DERBY
Tel: 01332 811400

Balloon Wood Adventure Playground
NOTTINGHAM
Tel: 0115 9150368

Beaumanor Park Outdoor Education Centre
LEICESTER
Tel: 01509 890119
Web: www.leics.gov.uk/educational/residential_services

Bumpi's Big Adventure
DERBY
Tel: 01332 204 292

Crazy Crocodiles
Abbey Street, Ilkeston, DERBYS
Tel: 0115 9441 555
All year round indoor adventure play centre for children 0 -10 yrs.

Crocodile Rock Childrens Centre
LEICESTER
Tel: 01664 501063

Denby Pottery Visitor Centre
on B6179, off A38, 2 miles south of Ripley, Denby, DERBYS
Tel: 01773 740700
Lot's of activities & entertainment, for children, during school holidays.

Freddy's Play Kingdom
50 Nottingham Road, Spondon, DERBY
Tel: 01332 662322
Childrens activity play and play centre. Discos, parties catered for-cafeteria serving food and drink.

Funky Pots
278/280 Huntington Street, NOTTINGHAM
Tel: 0115 9298025
Email: info@funkypots.co.uk
Web: www.info@funkypots.co.uk

Thus the Tumble Tots programme is designed to allow a child to achieve all that. The philosophy and purpose is to heighten through purposeful play:

- General Motor Skills,
- Social Awareness,
- Self-confidence,
- Self-discipline.

Tumble Tots - Its Objectives

Studies by educational psychologists show that a child's skills are enhanced if his or her levels of self-confidence, physical fitness and motor control are raised during the early formative and elementary years.

The basic premises of the need for the Tumble Tots programme are best described by English child psychologist, Alison Stallisbrass in her book, "The Self-respecting Child" (Pelican 1979).

 "Toddlers experience a strong desire to become acrobatically skilled."

 "This ability can be said to be necessary to a child's self-respect and feeling of self-worth."

"Nowadays a child's surroundings may not offer the opportunity to acquire it."

 "A child does not know what it needs unless the opportunities are present. He needs to start early, while his centre of gravity is still close to the ground to lay foundations of balance, agility and general physical co-ordination."

 "Owing to differences in temperament and physical build, some children find these skills easier to learn than others. There are differences too in the manner in which they respond to opportunities to climb, swing, jump and slide."

 "If children are to make the most of their opportunities, they must have the chance from the time they toddle, to climb up and down steps and stairs and slopes, to hang from their hands, and swing their legs, to bounce and tumble, to scramble and slide on their tummies."

 "This sort of play teaches more than balance, co-ordination and agility. The children are relying on their own judgement, taking decisions, sizing up the situation, becoming aware of their capabilities and limitations."

Tumble Tots provides a positive physical opportunity and environment where a child builds his progress. Achievement is derived from progress as success upon success builds confidence. Tumble Tots offers children joy, challenge and satisfaction.

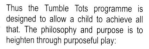
Tumble Tots Programme Concept

Tumble Tots is designed to build children's self-confidence by helping to develop the physical and social skills of pre-school children. This is done through the use of Tumble Tots brightly coloured proto-type equipment. Bars, trestles, balance ards, ladders, ball and hoops are used tasks assigned to include all aspects of ysical motor education for example ball handling, locomotive skill development, rhythms, manipulative skills etc. Coupled with the positive-laden, loving and caring Tumble Tots environment, the programme heightens a child's total body awareness.

Through the careful study of child behaviour during their formative years, the Tumble Tots programme is progressive in its methods. Because it recognises the emotional changes and stages in a child's life, each session is structured to cater to the different physical skill levels, behaviour and emotions of the age group. Thus Gymbabes and Tumble Tots in the walking to two-year-old and two-to-three-year-old class are accompanied by Mum, Dad or a Guardian that is someone the child is familiar with and who will fully participate in the sessions with the child.

Once a child is three, and much more aware of his physical capabilities, he is confident and independent and therefore goes through the Tumble Tots sessions unaccompanied. Children of this age group start to learn listening skills and follow instructions, while tacking more difficult tasks.

Trained staff supervise each Tumble Tots session with the staff ratio being one staff to six children, except for Gymbobs where the ratio is one staff to eight children. The maximum number of children in a class is 24.

Through Tumble Tots, children start to enjoy physical skills and are encouraged to explore and reach their maximum in physical skill capabilities. The programme also helps in a child's language development as they participate in action songs and rhymes.

Tumble Tots builds children's confidence as they learn to enjoy physical tasks, preparing them for Physical education or Gymnastics education during their school years.

Tumble Tots...
The Different Age Groups

The Tumble Tots programme develops a child's motor and mental skills during their formative years. This is recognised to be between 12 months and five years. The programme serves to prepare a child for his school years, with sessions for children of different age groups. Tasks are assigned according to the capabilities of each age group, which also allows children of the same age to socialise. Sessions are 45-minutes, once a week, and run at more than 500 centres in the United Kingdom.

Gymbabes
(six months to walking)

The youngest age group of the Tumble Tots programme, the Gymbabes programme offers babies an opportunity to socialise in an environment that enables their natural abilities of exploring, crawling and so on to flourish. The programme involves parents, who with guidance, help stimulate and encourage babies to use all their senses gently and without pressure.

Tumble Tots, walking to two-years

A class for children who have started to walk confidently, parents now turn their attention to encouraging their child to climb, jump, roll and other elementary physical activity which will stimulate their body awareness.

The Tumble Tots programme develops a child's motor and mental skills during their formative years.

Tumble Tots, two to three years

Sessions are based around "activity stations" which form the basis for various task sequences designed to enable children to develop their sense of balance, co-ordination and agility.

Tumble Tots, three years to school age

Class leaders focus on setting more challenging task sequences for building a child's co-ordination, ball skills, body awareness and controlled body movements. Collectively, a combination of activity features further develops children's confidence and social abilities.

Gymbobs, school age to seven years

These are for Tumble Tots graduates or children of school going age. Gymbobs offer children more challenging tasks. Gymbobs also learn to develop physical skills without using equipment and are introduced to the concept of teamwork and relays.

Tumble Tots National Club

All children attending Tumble Tots become members of the Tumble Tots National Club. The club is designed to instill in children a sense of belonging and identity. Children receive a membership pack which includes their membership T-shirt, annual subscription to Right Start Magazine, a host of privileges and are automatically insured whilst participating in Tumble Tots classes. Tumble Tots membership is valid at Tumble Tots centres internationally.

For more information, please ring Nivi Bhide of Tumble Tots (UK) Limi' on Tel: 0121-5857003.

Genesis Family Entertainment Centre
ALFRETON
Tel: 01773 52242

Goldhill Adventure Playground
LEICESTER
Tel: 0116 2836350

Hands On Pottery
NOTTINGHAM
Tel: 0115 9602892

Jumicar
Lowdham Leisureworld, Lowdham Road
Gunthorpe Bridge, NOTTINGHAM
Tel: 0115 9669000
Email: jumicar.notts@btopenworld.com
Web: www.btopenworld.com

Jumping Beans Fit kid Club
The Willows, Melton Mowbray,
LEICESTER
Tel: 07790 007713

Jungle Madness
SWADLINCOTE
Tel: 01283 551355

Funky pots is a fantastic new concept in Nottingham City Centre based on Huntingdon Street it is easily accessible by car, bus and tram.

The idea is delightful and just what is needed in the city centre to enable children and adults alike to escape the shopping mayhem, relax and explore their creative side.

Pottery pieces are available to purchase and you are then able to paint them (using lead free paints, of course) however you wish. The finished design is then left at the café to be "fired" in a kiln and collected a few days later. There are over 100 designs to choose from, including money boxes, cars, mugs, plates and children's characters. There are also seasonal designs for that extra special gift at Easter, Christmas or Halloween for example. Children as always love to play and enjoy creating a unique gift for a loved family member, friend or teacher. What better way to celebrate mother/fathers day than a hand crafted gift.

Birthday and other celebratory parties are catered for, which makes an interesting change as the children can make something to keep whilst sampling the café's scrumptious food selection. It is a unique way to explore new talents and a creative experience for the party-goers.

The proprietors, Mr & Mrs Tan have been running a mobile service in the East Midlands for several years and due to customer demand opened the pottery café earlier in the year. Their love of the subject and personable approach combines with the whole for an experience to remember.

Nursery and School parties are also welcomed, a mother and toddler group runs from the café or you can simply pop in. The premises are light and airy with disabled access and high chairs for the little artists.

inspire ... create ... paint ... enjoy

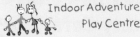
kool kids
Indoor Adventure
Play Centre

* Kool ball crawl   * Snooker tables
* Soft play ground   * Kool cafe
* Bouncy castle   * And much, much more!

Why not join the Kool Kids Club - Give us a call to find out more...
0115 9500125 - www.koolkids.biz
Carlton Road, Nottingham, NG3 2NR

Kool Kids Indoor Adventure Playcentre
Carlton Road, NOTTINGHAM
Tel: 0115 9500125

Lanky Bill's Fun Shack Ltd
NOTTINGHAM
Tel: 01773 767050

Manor Farm Animal Centre
Castle Hill, East Leake, Loughborough,
LEICESTER
Tel: 01509 852525

Paint a Pot
115 High Road, Beeston, NOTTINGHAM
Tel: 0115 9228029
A different and fun party for children of all ages at
Paint a Pot. Parties are 1 ½ hours long.

Paint a Pot
Markeaton Park Craft Village,
Markeaton Park
DERBY
Tel: 01332 202652
A different and fun party for children of all ages at
Paint a Pot. Parties are 1½ hours long.

PAINT YOUR OWN CERAMICS
Paint a Pot

We have a wide range of blank pottery shapes for
you to decorate. Great for any age and you don't
need any great artistic talent

Markeaton Park Craft Village
Markeaton Park, Derby
DE22 3BG. Tel: 01332 202652
11am - 4pm Mon Fri
10am - 5pm Sat & Sun

Now also open at
115 High Road, Beeston,
Nottingham. NG9 2LH
Tel: 01159 228029
10am - 5.30pm Tues - Sat
11am - 4.30pm Sun & Mon

planet happy
Play Centre

★ Large Adventure Play Frame.
★ Separate Area for Toddlers.
★ Parties from £6.95 per child.
★ Group Bookings and Private Hire.
★ Café serving Hot & Cold Food.
★ Toddler Sessions (term time only).

Open 7 days a week - 9:30am to 6:00pm
Admission £3 for two hours
Under 1's Free

Heage Road Industrial Estate,
Ripley, Derbyshire, DE5 3GH.
Tel. 01773 748600

Manor Farm
Animal Centre & Donkey Sanctuary

Open: weekends & Bank Holidays
(except 24th Dec to 2nd Jan)
10am - 5pm in Summer 10am - 4pm in Winter

Weekdays: Tues to Sun 10am - 4pm
Closed Mondays except Bank Holidays and above.

Children's Parties, Group visits & Seasonal Events

Early Years
Childcare Group

Castle Hill, East Leake,
Loughborough, Leics.
Tel: 01509 852525
www.manorfarm.info

INDOOR ADVENTURE PLAYGROUND

BIGGEST IN THE AREA

Open 7 days a week 10am - 5pm
Longer opening hours during winter

Ball pools • Soft Play Area • Glide & Slidey • Fit Balls • Separate Toddler Play Area • Mother & Toddler • Birthday Parties • Themed Parties

£2.30 one hour - £2.80 two hours
Play all day in term time for £2.80

Unit 1A Botany Commercial Park,
Botany Avenue, Mansfield, NG18 5NE
Telephone: (01623) 654 712

BRINGS THE OUTDOORS INDOORS

Play Island
DERBYS
Tel: 01332 875000

Planet Happy
Heague Road Ind Estate, Ripley,
DERBYS
Tel: 01773 748600

Playbarn
LEICESTER
Tel: 01858 432333

Playland
Unit 1a Botany Commercial Park
Botany Avenue, Mansfield, NOTTS
Tel: 01623 654712
*Indoor Play Centre, large under 3 area,
tots 2-10 yrs, parties and food available.*

Rushcliffe Arena
Rugby Road, West Bridgford,
NOTTINGHAM
Tel: 0115 9814027
*Childrens indoor soft play area and after school
club, great venue for children's parties.*

Scalliwags
Hilltop Mill, 49 Church Street, Earl Shilton
LEICESTER
Tel: 01455 840536

Smilee Faces
DERBYS
Tel: 01283 563999

Soccerama
DERBY
Tel: 01332 349193

St. Anns Playcentre
NOTTINGHAM
Tel: 0115 9584394

The Jungle Kingdom
LEICESTER
Tel: 0116 2661054

The Play Centre
NOTTINGHAM
Tel: 0115 9693432

The White Horse Inn
LEICESTER
Tel: 01455 28223

Treasure Island
NOTTINGHAM
Tel: 0115 9784836

Tumble Town Indoor Play Centre Ltd
NOTTINGHAM
Tel: 0115 9671161

Tumble Tots
Jayne Chadburn
NOTTINGHAM
Tel: 0115 9589767
Email: jayne.chadburn@tumbletots.com
Web: www.tumbletots.com/nottingham
Classes Gamstom, Keyworth, Long Eaton,
Radcliffe, West Bridgford.

Tumble Tots
Peter Rogers
NORTH NOTTINGHAM
Tel: 01623 635197
Email: peter.rogers@tumbletots.com
Web: www.tumbletots.com/northnottingham
Classes Mapperley, Mansfield Woodhouse,
Newark, Ravenshead

Tumble Tots
Smita Ghelani
LEICESTER WEST
Tel: 0116 2720057
Email: smita.ghelani@tumbletots.com
Web: www.tumbletots.com/leicesterwest
Classes Hinckley, Enderby, Glenfield, Lutterworth

Tumble Tots
Irene Jones
LEICESTER EAST
Tel: 0116 444555
Email: irene.jones@tumbletots.com
Web: www.tumbletots.com/leicestereast
Classes Market Harborough,
Melton Mowbray, Oadby

Tumble Tots
Wendy Campbell
LEICESTER EAST
Tel: 0116 444555
Email: wendy.cambell@tumbletots.com
Web: www.tumbletots.com/loughborough
Classes Ashby De La Zouch, Loughborough,
Measham, Rolleston-Burton, Whitwick

Twinlakes Park
Melton Spinney Road, Melton Mowbray, LEICESTER
Tel: 01664 567777
Email: mike@twinlakespark.co.uk
Web: www.twinlakespark.co.uk
Indoor & outdoor activities. Animals, action & fun. Farm &
rides for children from 2 yrs upwards. Must See!

Uppingham Summer School
LEICESTER
Tel: 01572 821264

Waterworld
DERBY
Tel: 1.78221e+009
Email: www.waterworld.co.uk

Acupuncture

Acupuncture & Herbal Medicine
LEICESTER
Tel: 01509 267431

Acupuncture and Chinese Herbal Medicine
NOTTINGHAM
Tel: 0115 9825353
Web: www.tcm-poplar.co.uk

Acupunture and Chinese Herbal Medicine
DERBY
Tel: 01332 605721

Acupunture by Roderick Edlin
DERBY
Tel: 01283 761795

Acupuncture Centre
DERBYS
Tel: 01332 763163

Acupuncture Clinic
DERBY
Tel: 01332 384136

Acupuncture Clinic
NOTTINGHAM
Tel: 0115 950 3231

Acupuncture Clinic
Mapperley Park, NOTTINGHAM
Tel: 0115 9623193

Ambion Acupuncture Clinic
LEICESTER
Tel: 01455 449309

A NEW VISION OF HEALTH
Dr. Carolyn Eddleston. GP and acupuncturist.

As I'm about to give birth to my first baby, I feel motivated to share with you my experience of using complementary therapies throughout my pregnancy. I write as a consumer and practitioner of Traditional Chinese Medicine (TCM). As a practitioner, I use acupuncture to support parents and children, bringing their bodies back to optimal health. I also work as a GP, so I stand comfortably between the two worlds of orthodox and complementary medicine.

Acupuncture, as part of TCM, is an ancient and complete system of medicine, having its own method of history taking, examination and diagnostic procedures. It is powerful in its effects and works well for couples having difficulty conceiving, period problems, recurrent miscarriages, and can also support the body whilst having IVF. I have been fortunate in having a normal pregnancy, and have continued to have regular acupuncture and reflexology which has supported me and the baby. My Acupuncturist will also be at the delivery to support us through all the stages of labour.

Acupressure techniques (no needles) can also be taught to parents as a preventative health routine for their baby and for specific problems such as colds, teething, and fevers.

More information on acupuncture is available on my website, **www.cyclesofchange.com.**

A NEW VISION OF HEALTH
Dr. Carolyn Eddleston
MBBS. MRCGP.DipAc.MBAcC
G.P and Acupuncturist

Cycles of Change Acupuncture Ltd
Loughborough Osteopathic Clinic
95, Ashby Rd.
Loughborough. LE11 3AB

www.cyclesofchange.com
Enquiries, Tel. 07980 904545
Appointments, Tel. 01509 262880

*My aim as a practitioner is to uplift people
I meet, activating wellbeing within them.*

Ann Dickinson MBAcC
DERBY
Tel: 01332 792808

Archway House Natural Health Centre
LEICESTER
Tel: 01858 410820

Beeston Natural Therapy Centre
NOTTINGHAM
Tel: 0115 9431 204

British Acupuncture Council
63 Jeddo Road, LONDON
Web: www.acupunture.org.uk
*All practitioner members of the British acupuncture Council
(BAcC) are fully qualified and observe stricts
codes of ethics and practice.*

C Topley
DERBYS
Tel: 01332 769488

Charnwood Chinese Medicine
LEICESTER
Tel: 01509 413111

Chinese Acupuncture & Herbal Clinic
LEICESTER
Tel: 0116 2559392

Chinese Herbal Mdicines & Acupuncture
LEICESTER
Tel: 0116 2538828

Coleman Road Contemplementary Therapy
LEICESTER
Tel: 0116 2599634

Cycles of Change Acupuncture
95 Ashby Road, Loughborough, LEICESTER
Tel: 01509 262880

Derby Chinese Medical Centre
DERBY
Tel: 01332 295700

Dianne Sadler
DERBYS
Tel: 01283 535006

Dr Beijung Chinese Remedies
DERBY
Tel: 01332 616199

Dr D A P Huggins
NOTTINGHAM
Tel: 0115 9397792

Dr.John Woodings M.B.Ch.B. DA Dip.Med.Ac
LEICESTER
Tel: 01572 822556

Five Element Acupunture
NOTTINGHAM
Tel: 07979 815759

Health Naturally
Charnwood Leisure Centre, Browns Lane,
LEICESTER, LE11 3HE
Tel: 01509 672708
*Acupuncture for well being during pregnancy and conditions
related to pregnancy. For appointments and further
information contact Caroline on 01509 672708.*

Joby Jackson
DERBYS
Tel: 01332 299133

Julie Dick
DERBY
Tel: 01332 380735

Katy Henry
DERBY
Tel: 01332 521270

Kegworth
LEICESTER
Tel: 01509 672457

Leicester Acupuncture Clinic
LEICESTER
Tel: 0116 2708149

Loughborough Osteopathic Clinic
LEICESTER
Tel: 01509 252880

Minerva Health Care
LEICESTER
Tel: 01455 282940

Richard Broughton D.C.H., C.H.I.R., MMSM
NOTTINGHAM
Tel: 0115 9605068

The Natural Way Health Centre
LEICESTER
Tel: 01509 261131

Traditional Chinese Acupuncture & Herbal
LEICESTER
Tel: 01162 712520
Fax: 01162 712520

Valerie Swinger MBAcC
DERBYS
Tel: 01283 221563

Wharf Practice
LEICESTER
Tel: 01858 464888

Adoption

Adoption - Nottingham City S/Services
NOTTINGHAM
Tel: 0115 9151234

Adoption and Fostering
DERBY
Tel: 01332 718000

11

Adoption

Adoption NCH Midlands
BIRMINGHAM
Tel: 0845 3555533
Web: www.nch.org.uk/adoption

Adoptionplus Ltd
BEDFORDSHIRE
Tel: 0116 2395267
Web: www.fosterplus.com

Barnados East Midlands Family Placement
DERBY
Tel: 01332 544711
Email: eastmidlands.fpc@barnados.org.uk
Web: www.barnados.org.uk

Children's Society
LEICESTER
Tel: 01509 600306

Families are Best
NOTTINGHAM
Tel: 0115 9558811

Five Rivers Family Placement Service
GLOUSTERSHIRE
Tel: 01332 638036

Foster Care Associates
BROMSGROVE
Tel: 01527 556480

Foster Care Associates
UTTOXETER
Tel: 01889 567516

Nottinghamshire Adoption Services
PO BOX 186, NOTTINGHAMSHIRE
Tel: 01623 476876

Airlines

Aer Lingus
Tel: 0845 084 4444
Web: www.aerlingus.ie

Air Canada
Tel: 0870 524 7226
Web: www.aircanada.ca

Air France
Tel: 0845 0845 111
Web: www.airfrance.co.uk

BMI Baby
Tel: 0870 6070 555
Web: www.flybmi.com

British Airways
Tel: 0845 850 9850
Web: www.britishairways.com

Easy Jet
Web: www.easy-jet.com

Quantas
Tel: 0845 774 7767
Web: www.quantis.co.uk

Ryanair
Tel: 0871 246 0000
Web: www.ryanair.com

Virgin Atlantic
Tel: 08705 747747
Web: www.virgin-atlantic.com

Alexander Technique

Ann Kestenbaum MSTAT
NOTTINGHAM
Tel: 0115 9602497

Association of Alexander Teachers
LEICESTER
Tel: 01455 891224
Web: www.paat.org.uk

Dr Mariam Wohl MB, ChB, JCCCert
LEICESTERSHIRE
Tel: 0116 2404243

Emmanuel Segerie
LEICESTER
Tel: 0116 2511647

Jenny Walsh
LINCOLNSHIRE
Tel: 01780 740991

Sally Rughani MSTAT
NOTTINGHAM
Tel: 0115 9609553

Sue Isaac
LEICESTER
Tel: 0116 2838510

Vivien Turner
LINCONSHIRE
Tel: 01780 753344

Yvonne White MSTAT
DERBY
Tel: 01332 521270

Announcement Cards

Cute as a button
Web: www.cuteasabutton.co.uk

Michael Clarke
Photography and Design
122 Hoe View Road, Cropwell Bishop,
NOTTINGHAM
Tel: 0115 9890532
Email: mac.photos@totalise.co.uk
Web: www.mcpd.net

Monkey Sites
Web: www.monkeysites.co.uk

Stork News
Web: www.storknews.co.uk

Ante-natal Support

Birth Matters
BELPER
Tel: 01773 826055
Email: diane@vizion.fsnet.co.uk
Web: www.vizion.fsnet.co.uk

The National Childcare Trust
Alexandra House, Oldham Terrace, Acton, LONDON
Tel: 0870 444 8707
Web: www.national-childbirth-trust.org.uk
The National Childbirth Trust (NCT) offers support in pregnancy, childbirth and early parenthood. There aim is to give every parent the chance to make informed choices. They try to make sure that all services, activities and membership are fully accessible.

Window To The Womb
The Laurels, Russell Avenue,
Wollaton, NOTTINGHAM
Ultrasound baby bonding scan studio.

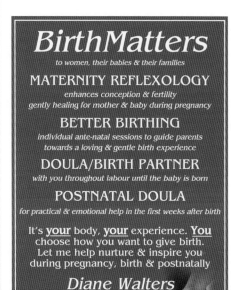

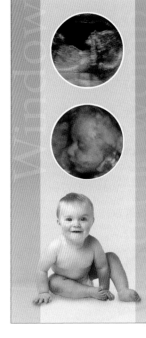
Aromatherapy

A Touch Better Natural Therapies
BURTON ON TRENT
Tel: 01283 562694

Alternative Health & Beauty
NOTTINGHAM
Tel: 0115 9665540
Email: havenalternative@aol.com
Web: www.aol.com

Angelic Aroma's
LEICESTER
Tel: 0116 2826749

AOC Organisations Council
NOTTINGHAM
Tel: 0115 9118416

Bernadette Spink
DERBY
Tel: 07813 586388
Caroline Gray I.T.E.C. V.T.C.T. MGPP
44 Nottingham Road, Keyworth, NOTTINGHAM
Tel: 0115 9373784
Complementary therapies including aromatherapy, stress massage, reflexology and hopi ear candles. Contact Caroline for an appointment.

Claire Hanson
LEICESTER
Tel: 0116 2991250

Clare Glover MIFPA, SPA
LEICESTER
Tel: 0116 2478645

Bramcote Leisure Centre
Derby Road, Bramcote, NOTTINGHAM, NG9 3GF
Tel: 0115 917 3000
Web: www.broxtowe.gov.uk

Aromatherapy

D Stevens
NOTTINGHAM
Tel: 0115 9118776

Dr Gillian Kemp
ALVASTON
Tel: 01332 571746

Essentia
LEICESTER
Tel: 0116 2992018

Face Up
DERBY
Tel: 01332 368195
Federation of Holistic Therapists
NOTTINGHAM
Tel: 0115 9825353

Feel Good Factor
LEICESTER
Tel: 0116 2778373

House of Aromatherapy
DERBY
Tel: 01332 202207
Keyholistic Therapies
NOTTINGHAM
Tel: 01773 780652

Larri Annis
DERBY
Tel: 01332 824488

Madina Aromatherapy & Reflexology
LEICESTER
Tel: 0116 2773723

Natural Health Therapist
LEICESTER
Tel: 0116 2895291

Purple Flowers Holistic Therapies
BURTON ON TRENT
Tel: 07736 299265

Robbie Simpson
LEICESTER
Tel: 0116 2717899

Thai Massage
LEICESTER
Tel: 01572 774354

The Natural Health Clinic
NOTTINGHAM
Tel: 0115 9810745

Touching Well
1 Mayfield Rd, Carlton Hill,
NOTTINGHAM
Tel: 0115 8457113
Email: info@touchingwell.co.uk
Web: www.touchingwell.co.uk
Pamper and nurture yourself,
soothe your back and shoulders,
feel calm, relaxed and alert - with
a touching massage.

BABY SHOWER TREND IS SWEEPING THE UK

A Cheshire businesswoman is looking across the Atlantic to help mums-to-be celebrate the imminent arrival of their bundles of joy. Suzanne Rudd, who lives in Stockton Heath, Cheshire, has imported the American tradition of 'baby showers' to the UK and hopes that expectant mothers and their friends and family will mark those last few weeks of pregnancy with a party to remember.

The mother of one has set up her own internet-based business – Baby Showers Galore – so that she can combine working with looking after one-year-old daughter Olivia. You can buy everything you need to throw an American-style baby shower on-line or can you invite Suzanne along to organise the event for you. The parties would also make an excellent 'goodbye' present for those mums-to-be finishing work to go on maternity leave and could easily be held in the workplace during the lunch hour.

> **A baby shower is the perfect way to brighten up those final days or weeks before baby arrives.**

There are four party themes to choose from and Baby Showers Galore can provide everything from invitations and tableware, to room decorations, balloons and party favors.
Baby showers have long marked the arrival of babies Stateside, but the trend is growing fast in this country with celebrities such as supermodel Kate Moss throwing a baby shower to mark the end of her pregnancy.

> **You find that many of your guests will have had children themselves and it is an ideal opportunity to get some last-minute tips and advice.**

Suzanne, 28, enjoyed her own baby shower just weeks before Olivia was born in March last year. She said: "The last few weeks of pregnancy can be really difficult. Mums-to-be are feeling fat, tired, fed-up – they need cheering up. A baby shower is the perfect way to brighten up those final days or weeks before baby arrives."

Traditionally, baby showers are attended by the female relatives and friends of the mum-to-be. Guests usually bring gifts for mother and baby, and offer words of wisdom to calm those nerves.

Suzanne, a former dental nurse, added: "Having a baby is the most wonderful event and it is really great to share the build-up with those close to you. You find that many of your guests will have had children themselves and it is an ideal opportunity to get some last-minute tips and advice."

You can find out more about holding a baby shower by visiting www.BabyShowersGalore.co.uk where you will find everything you need to make the party go with a swing. Suzanne can also be contacted directly on 01925 486632 or 07800 642695.

Baby Showers Galore

Development Baby Massage Classes
2 Dudley Doy Road, Southwell, NOTTINGHAM
Tel: 01636 819370
Email: chan@doctors.org.uk
Web: www.doctors.org.uk
5 week courses for babies from 6 wks old.

Touching Well
1 Mayfield Rd, Carlton Hill, NOTTINGHAM
Tel: 0115 8457113
Email: info@touchingwell.co.uk
Web: www.touchingwell.co.uk
Pamper and nurture yourself, soothe your back and shoulders, feel calm, relaxed and alert - with a touching massage.

Baby Sitters

Carol Shillington
DERBYS
Tel: 01773 783954

Claire Bostock
NOTTINGHAM
Tel: 0115 9626400

Heather White
DERBYS
Tel: 01773 782413

K Hawthorn
NOTTINGHAM
Tel: 0115 9855002

Linda Grice
NOTTINGHAM
Tel: 0115 9255024

Lindsey Swain
NOTTINGHAM
Tel: 01636 893280

R Samih
NOTTINGHAM
Tel: 0115 9743471

Rachel's Childminding
DERBYS
Tel: 0115 8540828

Safehands Network Ltd
RBC, Victoria Square, Cleveleys, LANCASTER
Tel: 0870 844 6688
Web: www.safehandsnetwork.com

Sitters Baby Sitting Service
126 Ricky Road, Watford, LONDON
Tel: 0800 3890038
Web: www.sitters.co.uk
Mature,reliable local babysitters with professional childcare experience. All carefully reference checked & interviewed in person. For more info call free on 0800 38 900 38.

Baby Showers

Home and Lifestyle Organiser
Reg Office: 1 Holles Crescent,
The Park, NOTTINGHAM
Tel: 0115 9475589
Web: www.haloltd.com
Providing Professional Lifestyle Solutions, Concierge Services, Personal Assistance, Home Renovations, Design and Project Management. See page 16.

Baby Signing

Tiny talk uk
NOTTS
Tel: 07971 847008

Balloons

Balloon Affair
DERBYS
Tel: 01283 542556

Balloon and Party ideas
DERBY
Tel: 01332 824268

Balloon and Party ideas
Nottingham
Tel: 0115`9242345

Pregnancy massage

During pregnancy a woman undergoes major physical and emotional changes. Massage offers a safe, natural and enjoyable way to increase the well being of both mother and foetus. Benefits of regular massage during pregnancy include:

- Massage is relaxing and therefore may prepare you for an easier delivery (or shall we say less difficult?) This may help you to approach your due date with less anxiety. The endorphins released by massage induce a deep relaxation that is also felt by your baby in the womb. Incidentally, midwives and doctors would agree that a relaxed mother is likely to have a happier and healthier pregnancy and possibly an easier birth experience.

- Massage will ease your physical discomfort by reducing pain in the lower back, pelvis and hips. Shoulder, neck and back strain due to postural changes are often relieved.

- Regular massage can increase muscle tone. This can help with muscle spasms and knots. At the same time the flexibility of ligaments, tendons and joints is maximized, this is particularly appreciated during labour.

- Massage increases the blood circulation to the entire body, including the placenta. This brings greater nutrition to the tissues and the foetus and enhances waste product removal.

- Swelling (oedema) of the feet, legs and hands is decreased. The lymphatic system is working more efficiently, resulting in less swelling and more energy for you.

- Massage can help to stabilize hormone levels, so the side effects of these hormones, such as morning sickness can be less severe.

There are many physical benefits of receiving regular massage during pregnancy; however, the emotional experience should not be ignored. The pregnant woman is doing a lot of nurturing – after all she is growing a baby – she can do with some nurturing herself!

Massage after the birth

Being a new parent is a shock to the system, albeit one most wouldn't exchange for anything in the world.

- Massage helps the body to adapt to the changes after the birth

- It eases sore shoulders and arms due from carrying your baby

- Massage is an opportunity for you to be nurtured at a time when you are doing a lot of nurturing yourself.

- Calms and relaxes you and therefore your baby

- Massage can't quite make up for interrupted night sleep, though you can leave refreshed and feeling that you can cope better

- Creates a feeling of well-being: you feel nurtured, in balance and alive

- Increased circulation, release of feel-good hormones, strengthened immune system and all the other benefits of massage.

You don't need to have a baby to enjoy the benefits of massage! My children are older now (and therefore a lot heavier to pick up) and I still enjoy regular massage – they do, too.

Infant massage is an ancient tradition in many cultures. It is being rediscovered in the West. Recent research shows that loving, touching and nurturing contact between caregiver and infant has an important impact on their development.

Baby massage

Infant massage is something that every parent or caregiver can learn and practice - providing benefits to both baby and parent. It consists of simple strokes using light natural oil to allow your hands to glide over baby's delicate skin. The movements are safe and relaxing for both you and the baby. Massage enables you to learn more about your baby's body language – and your baby gets to know you even better. It is one way to make your baby feel loved, secure and respected. Baby massage is something you do with, rather than to, your baby. The idea is that you have a good time together.

Other benefits of infant massage

• Helps to calm babies' emotions and relieve stress

• Soothes babies and help them to sleep better

• Helps babies to develop awareness of their body

• Aids digestion and helps to relieve colic, wind and constipation

• Helps to develop muscle tone, coordination and suppleness

• Strengthens the immune system

• Regulates breathing and relieves nasal congestion

• Improves skin texture

You can start massaging your baby from birth – or you can even go while pregnant. The best time to begin is between one and nine months before the baby starts crawling. Of course older children can also be massaged.

It is one way to make your baby feel loved, secure and respected.

You can learn from a book, individual teaching or a baby massage course. A baby massage course is sociable – you'll meet other (tired) parents, sharing the highs and lows of life with a new baby. You'll see that other babies can be just as delightful as yours – or as unhappy. A recent poll showed that 1 in 10 new parents feel isolated – a baby massage class is a good antidote for this. Many infant massage instructors are trained by the International Association of Infant Massage (.IA.I.M.). "The purpose of the I.A.I.M. is to promote nurturing touch and communication through training, education and research so that parents, caregivers and children are loved, valued and respected throughout the world community" (I.A.I.M. mission statement). Many courses run over five weeks with each weekly session lasting approximately one and a half hours. Classes are held in small groups of parents (or grand-parents or other carers) and babies. Participants massage their babies whilst being guided through a massage routine that uses a carefully balanced combination of Swedish, Indian and Reflexology techniques.

Regina Dengler from Touching Well is a Certified Infant Instructor (C.I.M.I.) trained with the I.A.I.M. She can be contacted on 0115 8457113, info@touchingwell.co.uk or www.touchingwell.co.uk.

Balloon Affair
DERBYS
Tel: 01283 542556

Balloon and Party ideas
DERBY
Tel: 01332 824268

Balloon and Party ideas
Nottingham
Tel: 0115 9242345

Balloon Heydays
DERBY
Tel: 01332 663693

Balloon Looney
Nottingham
Tel: 0115 9222520

Balloons by Party Creations
DERBY
Tel: 01332 207666

Celebration Balloons
DERBYS
Tel: 01332 872612

House Party
LEICS
Tel: 0116 2710100

Much More than Balloons
LEICESTER
Tel: 01530 414478

Streamers The Party People
Tel: 0870 163 5106

Book Clubs

Grolier
NORWICH
Tel: 0870 2404385

Book Shops

Ammanuel Christian Bookshop
NOTTINGHAM
Tel: 01636 700412

Beeston Bookshop
NOTTTINGHAM
Tel: 0115 9221631

Buythebook
NOTTINGHAM
Tel: 01636 613795

Buythebook
13 High Street, Oakham
Tel: 01572 723000

Christian Book Centre
NOTTINGHAM
Tel: 0115 9256961

County Book Shops
NOTTINGHAM
Tel: 0115 9722387

Frontline Books
73 Humberstone Gate, Leicester
Tel: 0116 2512002

Good News Centre
47 Churchgate, Loughborough
Tel: 01509 236057

Roving Books Ltd
Unit 3, Freehold Street, Leicester
Tel: 0116 25191513

Shepshed Books
14-20 Field St, Shepshed,
Tel: 01509 508929

The Book Café
15a St. Peters Way, Derby
Tel: 01332 204402

The Book Company
12 Market Street, Loughborough
Tel: 01509 235486

The Book Mark
1306 Melton Road, Syston
Tel: 0116 2693919

The Book Shop
16 Belvoir Road, Coalville
Tel: 01530 838771

The Minster Shop
NOTTS
Tel: 01636 812933

The Works
43 Market Place, Newark
Tel: 01636 700426

The Works
The Broad Marsh Centre, Nottingham
Tel: 0115 9509217

The Works
Victoria Centre, Nottingham
Tel: 0115 9581300

The Works
17 Octagon Centre, Burton On Trent
Tel: 01283 516783

The Works
115 St. Peters Street, Derby
Tel: 01332 293100

The Works
46-50 Gallowtree Gate, Leicester
Tel: 0116 2514976

The Works
12 Carillion Court, Loughborough
Tel: 01509 211288

Waterstone's
25 Wheeler Gate, Nottingham
Tel: 0115 9473531

Waterstone's
78-80 St Peter's Street, Derby
Tel: 01332 296997

Waterstone's
The Shires, Leicester
Tel: 0116 2516838

WHSmith
6 St. John St, Ashbourne
Tel: 01335 343109

WHSmith
28 Market Street, Ashby-de-la-Zouch
Tel: 01530 415588

WHSmith
13-17 Underhill Walk, Burton On Trent
Tel: 01283 565671

WHSmith
2 Devonshire Walk, Eagle Centre, Derby
Tel: 01332 364259

WHSmith
55 High Street, Long Eaton
Tel: 0115 9733875

WHSmith
36-38 Market Place, Newark
Tel: 01636 677518

WHSmith
24-26 Front Street, Arnold
Tel: 0115 9260656

WHSmith
25 High Street, Beeston
Tel: 0115 9222973

WHSmith
124-126 Victoria Centre, Nottingham
Tel: 0115 9470772

WHSmith
Fosse Park Shopping Centre, Leicester
Tel: 0116 2826443

WHSmith
Market Place, Melton Mowbray
Tel: 01664 562025

WHSmith
29-31 Castle Gate, Hinkley
Tel: 01455 891317

WHSmith
39 Gallowtree Gate, Leicester
Tel: 0116 2626252

WHSmith
9 Carillion Court, Loughborough
Tel: 01509 230424

WHSmith
13 High Street, Market Harborough
Tel: 01858 410540

Words of Discovery
Unit 33, Vulcan Road, Leicester
Tel: 0116 2622244

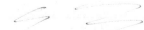

A Better Castle Hire
DERBY
Tel: 01332 557512

A1 Bouncy Acamdemy
DERBY
Tel: 01332 763326

Art Leisure
21 Balmoral Road, Colwick
NOTTINGHAM
Tel: 0115 9611567

Blaby Castle Hire
Leicester
Tel: 0116 2785026

Bouncy Castle Hire Co
DERBY
Tel: 01332 293600

Jack in the Box
50 Westwick Road, NOTTINGHAM
Tel: 0115 9138431
Fully insured bouncy castles for party hire, fetes and school.

Kiddies Kingdom
Tel: 01858 466553

Let's Bounce
DERBYS
Tel: 01283 551329

0700 2 Bounce Hire
Tel: 01509 853977

Breast Feeding

Association of Breastfeeding Mothers
Tel: 020 7813 1481
Breastfeeding support, covering the whole of the UK. When you call the above number they will give you a local contact in your area.

Breast Feeding Network
Tel: 0870 900 8787
Web: www.breastfeedingnetwork.co.uk
The telephone number and website are intended to provide support, reassurance and advice for anything to do with breast feeding. Call the national number and be connected to a local representative. There are also local meeting groups.

Le Leche League
Tel: 0845 120 2918
This support line aims to help mothers to breasetfeed through mother-to-mother support, encouragement, information and education.

The National Childcare Trust
Alexandra House, Oldham Terrace,
Acton, LONDON
Tel: 0870 444 8707
Web: www.national-childbirth-trust.org.uk
The National Childbirth Trust (NCT) offers support in pregnancy, childbirth and early parenthood. There aim to give every parent the chance to make informed choices. They try to make sure that all services, activities and membership are fully accessible

A Cake To Celebrate
NOTTINGHAM
Tel: 0772 932 2958

Beverley's Cakes
4 Gtange Drive, Long Eaton, NOTTINGHAM
Tel: 0115 9463198

Chocolate Art
MATLOCK
Tel: 01629 581291

Debbie Campbell
LEICESTER
Web: www.debbiecampbellcakes.co.uk

Delicious Dishes
DERBYS
Tel: 01283 550359

Helen Houlden Exclusive Cake Design
NOTTINGHAM
Web: www.helenhouldencakes.co.uk

Just Add Cake
NOTTINGHAM
Tel: 0115 953 7680

Sugar & Ice
LEICS
Tel: 01530 817210

Sweet Enough
128 Beckhampton Road,
Bestwood Park, NOTTS
Tel: 0115 8497956

Cards - Mail Order

Announce It
Tel: 020 8286 4044

Bambino Mio
Tel: 0870 770 8826

Chatter Box Cards
Tel: 020 8650 8650

Gossypium
Tel: 0870 777 0282
Email: catalogue@gossypium.co.uk

Greenfibres
Tel: 0845 330 3440
Email: mail@greenfibres.com

Little Green Earthlets
Tel: 01825 873301
Email: chris@littlegreenearthlets.co.uk

Castings

Life Casting Nottingham
10 Powtrell Place, Ilkeston,
NOTTINGHAM
Tel: 0115 9306772
Web: www.life-casting-uk.co.uk

Second Skin
40 Barrrow Road, Quorn,
Loughborough, LEICS
Tel: 01509 557393
Web: www.secondskin.uk.net

Childcare Services

Children's Information Service
DERBY
Tel: 01332 716381

Childcare Training

Childcare Study
4 Carnation Close, LEICESTER
Tel: 0116 2394779
Email: childcare@btinternet.com
Web: www.btinternet.com
Early years training and qualifications.

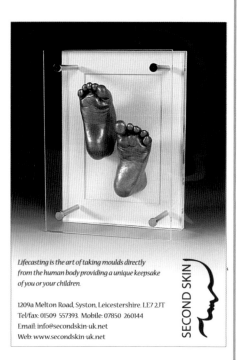

Amanda Jones
LEICESTER
Tel: 01455 447513

C Gibbons
DERBYS
Tel: 01332 518322
Fax: 1332

C Gutteridge
DERBY
Tel: 01332 833551

Cherubs Private Daycare
DERBYS
Tel: 01332 550329

Childrens Information Service
DERBY
Tel: 01332 716381

Cuddles Childminding Services
20 Mile End Road, Colwick, NOTTINGHAM
Tel: 0115 8470259
Email: victoria.ball3@ntlworld.com
Qualified nursery nurses providing care and
education for children 6 wks - 8 yrs before and
after school care

Fazila Latif
LEICESTER
Tel: 0116 2123309

Gill Wells
DERBYS
Tel: 01332 662583

Green S.
LEICESTER
Tel: 01509 556729

H Bell
NOTTINGHAM
Tel: 01949 875019

Humpty Dumpty Childminding
DERBY
Tel: 01332 764910

J Lewis
LEICESTER
Tel: 0116 2375376

Jane's Jolly Tots
Childminding Services
DERBY
Tel: 01332 741743

Little Acorns
4 Milton Close, Wigston, LEICESTER
Tel: 0116 2888510

M Clark
DERBYS
Tel: 01332 752773

Matthews Jayne Childcare
BURTON ON TRENT
Tel: 01283 815338

Mind That Child
LEICESTER
Tel: 01455 446302

Mrs Mary Gibson
DERBYS
Tel: 01332 348542

N Warden
LEICESTER
Tel: 0116 2991892

Play Away
Childminding Services
DERBYS
Tel: 01332 755192

Rebecca Bostock
Registered Childminder
DERBY
Tel: 01332 674680

Sarah Hamlyn
Registered Childminder
DERBY
Tel: 01332 602998

Sue's Childminding Services
DERBY
Tel: 01332 600456

Tots 2 Teens 2
DERBY
Tel: 01283 535883

Glitzy Girls is a top-to-toe make over for Girls between the ages of 5-12 years
19 Lincoln Drive, Mansfield Woodhouse, Nottingham. NG19 8JR. Tel: 01623 633963

Arty Antics
NOTTINGHAM
Tel: 0115 8401350
We offer an exiting Arty experience for girls and boys aged from 3 years upwards. Treat your child to a themed creative party at an affordable price. Make it a praty to remember and let the children create there own part bag, in which they can take home

Glitzy Girls Parties
19 Lincoln Drive, Mansfield, NOTTS.
Tel: 01623 633963
Web: www.glitzygirls.co.uk

Louby Lou
NOTTINGHAM
Tel: 0115 9130979
Face painting, hair braiding, balloon modeling for childrens parties

McArtney's Catering
26 Launceston Crescent, Wilford, NOTTINGHAM
Tel: 0115 8780271
Web: www.mcartneys.co.uk

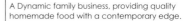

McArtney's Catering

A Dynamic family business, providing quality homemade food with a contemporary edge.

Canapes . Business Function
Dinner Parties . Smart Buffets . Weddings

26 Launceston Cresent, Wilford, Nottingham. NG11 7DN
Tel/Fax: 0115 8780271 . Mobile: 07771 902235
www.mcartneys.co.uk

Chiropracters

British Chiropratic Association
Web: www.chiropractic-uk.co.uk
Members of the BCA are fully qualified and abide by a strict code of ethics and are registered with the General Chiropractic Council and Doctors of Chiropractic.

Christening Gifts

Hot-hands
13 Malvern Road, West Bridgford, NOTTINGHAM
Tel: 0115 8781805
Web: www.hot-hands.co.uk
Your child's hands or foot prints individually portrayed on a uniquely designed and coloured canvas" recording their little size forever. Colours selected to suit home interior. Prices start from £29.00

Paint a Pot
115 High Road, Beeston, NOTTINGHAM
Tel: 0115 9228029
A different and fun party for children of all ages at Paint a Pot. Parties are 1 1/2 hours long.

Paint a Pot
Markeaton Park Craft Village, Markeaton Park, DERBY
Tel: 01332 202652
A different and fun party for children of all ages at Paint a Pot. Parties are 1½ hours long.

The Minster Shop
NOTTS
Tel: 01636 812933

Christening Wear

Christening Gowns
35 Derwent Crescent, Kettering,
NORTHANTS
Tel: 01536 515401
Web: www.christeningoutfits.co.uk
*Gowns, dresses, rompersuits and suits. Plus
accessories, including personalised bibs.*

Evolution
42 Oxford Street, Ripley, DERBYS
Tel: 01773 744553
Web: www.designerclothes4kids.co.uk
*Large selection of designer wear, including shoes,
gifts and christening wear.*

Junior B By Brigdens
54 Sadler Gate, DERBY
Tel: 01332 202373-384665
*Designer childrenswear including Burberry, DKNY,
Kenzo and more. Plus Christening Wear.*

Katherine Spillar
23 Mayfield Drive, NOTTINGHAM
Tel: 07930 178338

Little Gems
36 Bell Street, Wigston, LEICESTER
Tel: 07970 926194
*Little Gems have just moved to Wigston where they
have a selection of designer wear for babies and
children. They also stock christening wear.*

Militia Immaculatae Trust
LEICESTER
Tel: 0116 2513477
Web: www.mitrust.org

Piccolo
16 High Steet, Edwinstone, NOTTINGHAM
Tel: 01623 824000
*Designer childrens's wear and communion and
christening wear specialists.*

Cinemas

Metro Cinema
DERBY
Tel: 01332 340170

Piccadilly Cinema
LEICESTER
Tel: 0116 251 8880

Showcase Cinema
NOTTINGHAM
Tel: 0115 9866766
DERBY
Tel: 01332 270300

UCI
DERBY
Tel: 0870 0102030

UGC Cinemas
NOTTINGHAM
Tel: 0871 200 2000

Warner Village Cinema
LEICESTER
Tel: 0870 2406020

Accessories designer Katherine Spiller has a serious shoe habit. Lucky, then, that she makes them herself. 'I am obsessed with shoes. I've got 200 pairs, although 90 of those are my own designs!' It's these seriously sexy creations that are marching the vivacious 31 year old right to the top of the fashion world, earning her a celebrity clientele to die for. However not satisfied with designing

women's shoes Katherine has now launched her award winning range of children's christening dresses and baby shoes. You only need to take one look at this gorgeous range to fully understand why, when it comes to innovative baby shoe design, Baby Walker's are way ahead of the competition. The latest collection entitled "Angels with dirty faces" is inspirational and radically different from anything else in the market place. Katherine is working in partnership with Swells Maternity Wear, who already offer a personal shoe fitting service for their toddlers making these adoring baby shoes a must for all mums to be and parents alike, who want comfortable and practical baby shoes with that added wow factor in unique design. Baby Walkers not only offer comfort and durability but also the revolutionary drop-hi-tech lining which is breathable, absorbs perspiration of the foot and is antibacterial. It is the only baby shoe "in the market place" of its kind to offer this revolutionary lining.

Accessories designer Katherine Spiller has a serious shoe habit. Lucky, then, that she makes them herself. 'I am obsessed with shoes. I've got 200 pairs, although 90 of those are my own designs!

Baby Walkers not only offer comfort and durability but also the revolutionary drop-hi-tech lining which is breathable, absorbs perspiration of the foot and is antibacterial. It is the only baby shoe "in the market place" of it's kind to offer this revolutionary lining.

Katherine Spiller

Made from the softest Italian leather in an array of colours and styles, the collection is a noticeable move away from the image of children wearing typical black patent shoes. So who will the new collection appeal to? Baby Walkers sales and marketing director Cate Moss explains: "Our designs and service ethos is simple: to go beyond anything you might expect from even the best brands in the market place."Having evolved from a design background, Baby Walkers continues to bring this creative thinking into children's shoe design, ensuring you receive original concepts and powerful design statements. Working closely with the client , Katherine's personal design service ensures all your needs and expectations are catered for, right through to your doorstep. Our drive and passion maintain our standards and our focus is to offer you the very best in designer baby shoes. As a special limited edition promotion, Katherine is offering you the chance to view her exquisite, tailor made christening dresses from her Baptism collection . Available in Silk, Chiffon and Satin, they are a must for all occasions, from christening to weddings. Her eye catching collection has already caught the attention of buyers from the top bridal boutiques and department stores nationwide.

Stockist details: Baby Walker's limited edition range can be viewed at Swells maternity Wear in Nottingham's Broad Marsh Centre, tel: 0115 947 0408, open 7 days. For all other stockists of christening dresses & mail order catalogues please contact Cate at the press office on mobile: 079301 78338.

Clean Living
2 Exbourne Road, Aspley, NOTTINGHAM
Tel: 07963 749 273
Email: cleanliving2004@ntlworld.com

Merry Maids
3 Stadon Road, LEICESTER
Tel: 0116 234 1000
Web: merrymaids@
wecleanleicester.demon.co.uk
*Merry Maids will clean your home weeky,
fortnightly, monthly, on speacial occasions or
whenever you need us. All staff carry ID badges,
are uniforms & fully trasined, courteous and
flexible.*

Poppies of Nottingham
Dadley Road, Charlton-In-Lindrick, Worksop
Tel: 0115 967 9292

Poppies of Derby
Unit 2, Burton Enterprise Centre, Waterloo St,
Burton-on-Trent
Tel: 01283 741449

Quality 1st Cleaning
NOTTINGHAM
Tel: 0115 9868427

Clothing Shops

Adams Childrenwear Ltd
WARWICKSHIRE
Tel: 02476 351000

Aileen Penn
DERBY
Tel: 01332 341927

Angels
DERBYS
Tel: 01332 814599

Anju Fashions
LEICESTER
Tel: 0116 2611182

Babyco
LEICS
Tel: 01530 830066

Balloons Childrenswear
NOTTINGHAM
Tel: 0115 9455829

Ballyhoo
LEICESTER
Tel: 0116 2627566

Beli Bambini
LEICESTER
Tel: 01858 465179

Bitz for Kidz
STAFFS
Tel: 01889 565515

Bon Nuit Ltd
NOTTINGHAM
Tel: 01636 642834
Web: www.bon-nuit.com

Boomerang
NOTTINGHAM
Tel: 01476 578581

Carela
DERBYS
Tel: 01773 820648

Cashe
10 Greyhound Street, NOTTINGHAM
Tel: 0115 9411617
A treasure trove of designer labels in a new city-centre location. Three floors for ages 0-16 yrs. Stockists of Burberry, Moschino, Armani, Polo Ralph Lauren, Gant, DKNY, Timberland and D&G.

Children's Choice
17 Bridge Street, Belper, DERBYS
Tel: 01773 825865
Specialists in schoolwear. Official scout and guide shop, children's fashions from newborn to teens. Nursery equipment. Everything you need for your baby!

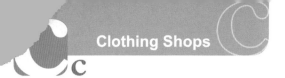

Christening Gowns
35 Derwent Crescent, Kettering,
NORTHANTS
Tel: 01536 515401
Web: www.christeningoutfits.co.uk
Gowns, dresses, rompersuits and suits.
Plus accessories, including personalised bibs.

Clafoutis
25 Loseby Lane, LEICESTER
Tel: 0116 2627027
Visit Clafoutis to find good selections of popular designer names.

Country Mouse Mrs Lander
LEICS
Tel: 01530 411844

Crucial Clothing Ltd
LEICESTER
Tel: 0116 2124149

De Bradelei Mill Shop Ltd
BELPER
Tel: 01773 829840

CLAFOUTIS

Designer childrens clothing
0-14years

RALPH LAUREN . MINIMAN . CATIMINI . DIOR
. ESCADA . DKNY . CHIPIE . KOOKAI . OXBOW
WILD SOUTH . KICKERS . REPLAY . PONY

25 Loseby Lane, Leicester 0116 2627027

Dirty Paws
STOKE
Tel: 01636 525052

Early Times
DERBYS
Tel: 01332 541561

Ekko Designer Wear
BURTON-ON-TRENT
Tel: 01283 566642

Ethel Austin Ltd
NOTTINGHAM
Tel: 0115 9760831

Ethel Austin Ltd
DERBYS
Tel: 01283 212706

Evington Stores
LEICESTER
Tel: 0116 2738311

Evolution
42 Oxford Street, Ripley, DERBYS
Tel: 01773 744553
Web: www.designerclothes4kids.co.uk
Large selection of designer wear, including shoes, gifts and christening wear.

Family Warehouse
LEICS
Tel: 01530 262274

Florence Davys
NOTTINGHAM
Tel: 0115 9732903

Heanor Family Care
DERBYS
Tel: 01773 767074

Hewitts The Childrens Shop
DERBYS
Tel: 01283 568870

Jazz
NOTTINGHAM
Tel: 01773 760090

Jellyrolls
25 Francis Street, LEICESTER
Tel: 0116 2704277

Jellyrolls Footwear
10 St. Martins Square, LEICESTER
Tel: 0116 2425222

Jellyrolls Kidswear
33 Silver Street, LEICESTER
Tel: 0116 2519500

Jellyrolls Nursery
35 Silver Street, LEICESTER
Tel: 0116 2623503

Jo Jo Maman Bebe
Distribution House, Oxwich Road,
Newport, SOUTH WALES
Tel: 0870 241 0560
Web: www.jojomamanbebe.co.uk
Extremely Stylish maternity wear at reasonable prices, plusl underwear, nursery goods and children's clothing.

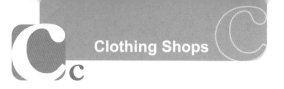

Junior B By Brigdens
54 Sadler Gate, DERBY
Tel: 01332 202373-384665
Designer childrenswear including Burberry, DKNY, Kenzo and more. Plus Christening Wear.

Kaos
LEICESTER
Tel: 01572 722601

Kids at Scotney's
132 London Road, LEICESTER
Tel: 0116 2556942
Web: www.christopherscotney.co.uk

Kids Kit
NOTTINGHAM
Tel: 0115 9631037

Kids Save
BURTON-ON-TRENT
Tel: 01283 517534

Kids Talk
NOTTINGHAM
Tel: 0115 9261962

Kidzone Ltd
3 Burton Street, Melton Mowbray, LEICESTER
Tel: 01664 500100
Quality schoolwear & fashion from pre-school to teens.

Kurmi
NOTTINGHAM
Tel: 0115 9121038

Little Gems
36 Bell Street, Wigston, LEICESTER
Tel: 07970 926194
Little Gems have just moved to Wigston where they have a selection of designer wear for babies and children. They also stock christening wear.

Little Rascals
NOTTINGHAM
Tel: 01636 613860
Web: www.littlerascalsdesignerwear.co.uk

Little Star
LEICESTER
Tel: 01455 616028

Martins School Wear
NOTTINGHAM
Tel: 0115 9874315

Mary's Childrenswear Eagle Centre
DERBY
Tel: 01332 381158

Michael De Leon
LEICESTER
Tel: 0116 2629371

Mothercare Uk Ltd
BURTON ON TRENT
Tel: 01283 567 472

Mothercare Uk Ltd
DERBYS
Tel: 01332 280570

Mothercare Uk Ltd
NOTTS
Tel: 01636 701695

Mothercare World
DERBYS
Tel: 01332 280750

Mothercare World
NOTTINGHAM
Tel: 0115 9240870

Munchkins
NOTTS
Tel: 01636 813040

National Schoolwear Centres
LEICESTER
Tel: 0116 2855077

Niche
NOTTINGHAM
Tel: 0115 9731901

Oilily at Jellyrolls
18 Francis Street, LEICESTER
Tel: 0116 2709129

PCz Designer Wear for Kids
159/161 Nottingham Road, Arnold, NOTTINGHAM
Tel: 0115 9670818
Large selection of designer wear for babies,
children and young mums. Car park at rear.

Penn Aileen
DERBY
Tel: 01332 341927

Piccolo
16 High Steet, Edwinstone, NOTTINGHAM
Tel: 01623 824000
Designer childrens's wear and communion and
christening wear specialists.

Pumpkin Patch Ltd
19a The Eagle Centre, Albion Street,
DERBY
Tel: 01332 348735

Rainbow Kids
LEICESTER
Tel: 0116 2812945

Rig-Out Childrens Wear
NOTTINGHAM
Tel: 0115 9255181

Scotney Kids
132 London Road, Leicester
Tel: 0116 255 6942

Shoe-Be-Doo
LEICESTER
Tel: 01572 821933

Smartipants Designer Wear
DERBY
Tel: 01332 541129
Web: www.smartipants.co.uk

Swifts - The Uniform People
LEICESTER
Tel: 01455 238398

The Big Rock Designer Store
NOTTINGHAM
Tel: 07775 604878
Web: www.bigrockmailorder.co.uk

The John Cheatle Group
LEICESTER
Tel: 0116 2990909

The Rival
LEICESTER
Tel: 0116 2513866

The Rocking Horse Clothing Company
NOTTINGHAM
Tel: 01773 785401

The Stork
LEICESTER
Tel: 01664 564215

Tick Tock Childrens Wear
LEICESTER
Tel: 01509 211944

Toffs
LEICESTER
Tel: 01572 724133

Togs & Toggles
NOTTINGHAM
Tel: 0115 9754808

Togs & Toys
NOTTINGHAM
Tel: 0115 9811257

Tots 2 Teens
23 Nottingham Road, Stapleford,
NOTTINGHAM
Tel: 07977 649675
New & nearly new childrens wear.
Top brands bourght and sold.

Trendy Schoolwear
LEICESTER
Tel: 0116 2767638

Trendy Tots
DERBY
Tel: 01773 821260

Wild Child
LEICESTER
Tel: 0116 2235990

Wise Owl Childrens Wear
DERBY
Tel: 01332 553392

Yusuf Fashions
LEICESTER
Tel: 0116 2626942

Zara (UK) Ltd - kids
NOTTINGHAM
Tel: 0115 9348780

Allestree Before and After School Club
DERBY
Tel: 01332 737947

Austin Community Enterprise Ltd
DERBY
Tel: 01332 774264

Braunstone Adventure Playgroup
LEICESTER
Tel: 0116 2919700

Castle Playgroup
LEICESTER
Tel: 0116 2394772

Costock Playgroup
LEICESTER
Tel: 01509 856387

Edwalton & Gamston Kids Club
Scout Hut, Alford Road, Edwalton, NOTTINGHAM
Tel: 07721 407300
Before and after school care and holiday clubs,
4-12 yrs. Various play and craft activites.

First Class Day Nursery
Parkland Primary School Grounds,
St. Thomas Road, South Wigston, LEICESTER
Tel: 0116 2778829
Web: www.firstclassnursery.co.uk
Full time and part time places available all
year round, including term time funded places for
3-4 year olds. We also charge hourly rates not
sessional!

Kiddy Shack
NOTTINGHAM
Tel: 0115 840 4476

Mellor Play Group
LEICESTER
Tel: 0116 2611211

Phoenix After School & Holiday Club
BURTON-ON-TRENT
Tel: 01283 226518

Pierrepont Gamston Kids Club
2 Silver How Close, West Bridgford,
NOTTINGHAM
Tel: 07721 407300
Email: sally@kidsclub@hotmail.com
Web: www.kidsclub@hotmail.com

Scalliwagz Ltd
DERBYS
Tel: 01283 730863

Scout Association
LONDON
Tel: 0845 3001818
Web: www.scoutbase.org.uk

Silvertrees Kids Club
NOTTINGHAM
Tel: 0115 973 2311

The Girls Guide Association
LONDON
Tel: 0207 8346242
Web: www.guides.org.uk

The Great Dalby Pre-School Playgroup
LEICESTER
Tel: 01664 411819

The Scout Association
Tel: 0115 9523617
Email: office@nottinghamshire-scouts.com
Web: www.nottinghamshire-scouts.com

Topsham House Childrens Club
LEICS
Tel: 01455 828855

Whitehouse Kids Club
DERBYS
Tel: 01332 820404

Concerts

Nottingham Arena
Bolero Square, The Lace Market,
NOTTINGHAM
Tel: 0870 121 0123
Web: www.nottingham-arena.com
24 hr ticket hotline 0870 121 0123.
Family shows, concerts and sporting events.

The Royal Centre
Theatre Square, NOTTINGHAM
Tel: 0115 989 5555

The Royal Centre

The Royal Centre plays host to a large number of family orientated shows throughout the year in both the Theatre Royal and Royal Concert Hall. These including our annual festive pantomime, classical ballet, adaptations of best-selling children's books and many of your favourite children's shows and entertainers who regularly appear on the television.

For more information on family shows which are currently on sale and the discounts available for children and families visit our website at www.royalcentre-nottingham.co.uk or call the Box Office on (0115) 989 5555.

Concierge Services

Home and Lifestyle Organiser
Reg Office: 1 Holles Crescent The Park,
NOTTINGHAM
Tel: 0115 9475589
Web: www.haloltd.com
*Providing Professional Lifestyle Solutions,
Concierge Services, Personal Assistance, Home
Renovations, Design and Project Management.*

Lifestyle Management (UK) Ltd
Unit 2b, 26-30 Stoney Street,
The Lace Market, NOTTINGHAM
Tel: 0115 9410 889
Web: www.lifestylemanagementuk.com

Cookery

The Manor School of Fine Dining
NOTTINGHAM
Tel: 01949 81371

Cord Blood Storage

UK Cord Blood Bank
BUCKINGHAMSHIRE
Tel: 01494 786117
Web: www.cordbloodbank.co.uk

Councils

Amber Valley
Tel: 01773 570222

Ashfield
Tel: 01623 450000

Bassetlaw
Tel: 01909 533533

Blaby
Tel: 0116 2750555

Bolsover
Tel: 01246 240000

Broxtowe
Tel: 0115 9177777

Charnwood
Tel: 01509 263151

Chesterfield
Tel: 01246 345345

Derby City
Tel: 01332 293111

Derbyshire County Council
Tel: 01629 580000

Derbyshire Dales
Tel: 01629 580580

Erewash
Tel: 0115 9461321

Gedling
Tel: 0115 9013901

Harborough
Tel: 01858 410000

High Peak
Tel: 01457 851600

Hinkley and Bosworth
Tel: 01455 248141

Leicester
Tel: 0116 2549922

Home & Lifestyle Organisers Ltd

Whether you are a Mum-To-Be or New Mum...
...everyone needs an extra pair of hands

Mums-To-Be

∂   No time to research the best buggy, car seat or cot?
∂   Rather not endure the discomfort of endless shopping trips?
∂   Is the nursery still not decorated?

HALO can help with all these things. Whether you haven't got the time or simply don't want the hassle, give HALO your brief and we'll do the hard work for you.
You can then concentrate on looking after yourself and your baby.

New Mums & Dads

Those first few days and weeks can be a daunting prospect, even for the most organised new mum and dad. Why not let HALO facilitate the arrival home of your new baby? We'll take care of those time-consuming, everyday tasks, so you can focus on your new family addition. We can also organise flowers, thank yous and the perfect christening.

∂   Shopping – Your fridge is always full
∂   Cleaning – Forget about the housework
∂   Cooking – Home-cooked delights delivered to your door

HALO is the one-stop shop for all your home and lifestyle needs!

Tel: 0115 986 1533   Email: info@haloltd.com   Website: www.haloltd.com

Home & Lifestyle Organisers Ltd

Leicestershire County Council
Tel: 0116 2323232

Mansfield
Tel: 01623 463463

Melton
Tel: 01664 567771

Newark and Sherwood
Tel: 01636 605111

North West Leicestershire
Tel: 01530 454545

Nottingham City
Tel: 0115 9155555

Nottinghamshire County Council
Tel: 0115 9823823

Oadby and Wigston
Tel: 0116 2888961

Rushcliffe
Tel: 0115 9819911

South Derbyshire
Tel: 01283 221000

Counsellors

Becky Goddard
NOTTINGHAM
Tel: 0115 9141616
Email: becky.goddard@ntlworld.com
Web: www.ntlworld.com

Craniosacral Therapy

Craniosacral Therapy Association
Tel: 07000 784735
Web: www.craniosacrel.co.uk

Jenny Meadows
DERBYS
Tel: 01773 873747

Pat Hughes
354 Mansfield Road, Carrington, NOTTINGHAM
Tel: 0115 9608855
Also at the Optimum Health Centre, 26a Central Avenue, West Bridgford, Nottingham NG2 5GR -
Tel: 0115 9143311.

Benefits of Craniosacral Treatment for babies

- Helps babies to feel relaxed, calm & content
- Improves feeding: eases painful wind & colic
- Improves Sleep: Less disturbed sleep, less irritability and restlessness
- Strengthens immune system: eases coughs, colds, and chest and ear infections.
- Helps skin problems
- Helps baby to recover from the shock of a very quick, a prolonged or a different birth, by calming and soothing the nervous system.

Case Study:

Bobby, a first child aged 6 weeks, had a very long labour and a forceps delivery. He was a restless feeder, very irritable with a lot of wind, colic and constipation. Sleep was very light and disturbed at night.

On examination I found some compression of the head and neck, due to the length of time and position Booby was inside the birth canal. This caused tension to the cranial nerves that supply the digestive system and affected his ability to deal with wind. His whole body felt quite tight and contracted especially around his diaphragm, this is a typical reaction to shock.

I concentrated on releasing the tension in his body, with a very gentle pressure on specific parts of the head and spine. Bobby went into a deep sleep for most of the 30 minutes I worked and his mother reported that later he was feeding better, the colic had eased and he filled his nappy. Over 2 further sessions Bobby continued to improve and he relaxed more deeply. His sleep improved and he was generally more contented.

Creche Hire

Scalliwags
LEICESTER
Tel: 0116 2813469
Email: scalliwags2002@aol.com

118 Dance Club
LEICESTER
Tel: 0116 2517073

A Culley
NOTTS
Tel: 0115 9633428

A.B.C. Ballroom
LEICESTER
Tel: 0116 2530463

A1 Dance Centre
NOTTINGHAM
Tel: 01773 762177

Absolute Salsa
DERBY
Tel: 0800 9707859

Anima Dance
LEICESTER
Tel: 0116 2708743

Ashworth School of Dance and Drama
NOTTINGHAM
Tel: 0115 9312573

Assemble School of Dancing
LEICESTER
Tel: 0116 2367308

Belly Dance For All
DERBY
Tel: 01332 367444

Bromage-Webster School of Dance
NOTTINGHAM
Tel: 0115 9256661

Cabaret Theatre School
DERBYSHIRE
Tel: 01332 518422

Caberet Theatre School
DERBYS
Tel: 01332 518422

Ceroc Central
NOTTINGHAM
Tel: 0800 1976248

Charlotte Hamilton School of Dance
NOTTS
Tel: 01636 684750

Charnwood School Of Dance
LEICESTER
Tel: 01509 412663

Christine Dunbar School of Dancing
NOTTINGHAM
Tel: 01509 672062

Christine March Dance School
NOTTS
Tel: 01623 458282

Dance Doctors Studios
NOTTINGHAM
Tel: 0115 9464822

Dance Doctors Studios
NOTTINGHAM
Tel: 0115 9464822
Email: info@dancedoctors.co.uk
Web: www.dancedoctors.co.uk

Dance Gear Direct
WEST MIDLANDS
Tel: 0121 420 1999

Dance Network
LEICESTERSHIRE
Tel: 01530 262248

Dance Sensation
LEICESTER
Tel: 0116 2920734

Dance Zone Studios
NOTTINGHAM
Tel: 0115 9162006

Dancetek
DERBY
Tel: 01332 720750

Dancing at Desford
LEICESTER
Tel: 01455 822022

Dawn King Ballet School
Gedling Memorial Hall, Main Road,
Gedling, NOTTINGHAM
Tel: 0115 9554164
Web: www.gedlingballetschool.co.uk
Dance classes for children from 3 years.
RAD registered teacher.

Derby Academy School
DERBYS
Tel: 01332 371016

Derby Dance Centre
DERBY
Tel: 01332 370911

Devas
LEICESTER
Tel: 01509 880120

Diane Fleming RAD Teaching DIP
DERBYS
Tel: 01773 745108

Dixon Woods School of Dance
LEICESTER
Tel: 0116 2434021

Drummondance
LEICESTER
Tel: 0116 2403000

Duet Academy of Dance
LEICESTER
Tel: 0116 2750881

Dupont Dance Stage School
LEICESTER
Tel: 0116 2629229

**Echoes of Erin
School of Irish Dancing**
DERBY
Tel: 01332 776461

Edmar School of Dancing
LEICESTER
Tel: 0116 2881943

Enderby Institute
LEICESTER
Tel: 0116 2848943

Expressions Dance Academy
LEICESTERSHIRE
Tel: 01530 836663

Expressions Dance Studio
LEICESTER
Tel: 01530 836663

First Stage
DERBY
Tel: 01332 701295

Footlights Dancing Schoool
DERBY
Tel: 01332 721108

Gedling Ballet School
NOTTINGHAM
Tel: 0115 9554164

Grace School of Dance
LEICESTER
Tel: 0116 2898080

Gracedieu Academy of Dance
LEICESTER
Tel: 01455 283856

Greek Dancing
NOTTINGHAM
Tel: 0115 9231070

Gymnastic & Dance Academy
LEICESTER
Tel: 0116 2826604

**Harborough Academy of
Performing Arts**
Hollies Fleckney Road, Kibworth
LEICESTER
Tel: 0116 2792194

Harlequin Dance School
LEICESTER
Tel: 0116 2674775

Hughes School of Dance
DERBY
Tel: 01332 780014

IBC School of Dancing
NOTTINGHAM
Tel: 0115 8495275

Imperial Academy of Dance
LEICESTER
Tel: 0116 2786064

Jane Hollingsworth
LEICESTER
Tel: 01572 737795

**Jill Gregory
School of Dancing**
DERBYS
Tel: 0115 9327495
Email: jill@mee-gregory.freeserve.co.uk
Web: www.mee-gregory.freeserve.co.uk

Joan Ross School of Dancing
DERBYS
Tel: 01283 212332

**Kerry Ledger
School of Dancing**
DERBYS
Tel: 0115 9308564

Kibworth Dance Centre
LEICESTER
Tel: 0116 2793981

**Kids & Co
School of Dancing**
NOTTINGHAM
Tel: 01636 688681

L & B Line Dancing
DERBYS
Tel: 01332 370824

Leicester Dance Company
LEICESTER
Tel: 01455 282837

Leonard School of Dance Ltd
24 Leahurst Road, West Bridgford,
NOTTINGHAM
Tel: 0115 9234115
*Royal Academy of Dance registered School
offering classical ballet for children from 3 yrs up
to advanced.*

Linda Cook School Of Theatre Dance
DERBYS
Tel: 01332 572387

Linda William Academy of Dance
LEICESTER
Tel: 01455 822022

Little Bowden School of Dancing
LEICESTER
Tel: 01858 461316

Loughborough School of Ballet
LEICESTER
Tel: 0116 2302010

**Louisa Holmes
School for Performing Arts**
NOTTINGHAM
Tel: 0115 9624648

Lynroys Dancing School
LEICESTER
Tel: 01509 216066

Marcia Jones School of Dance
NOTTINGHAM
Tel: 0115 9857961

Marjorie Wise School of Dance
St Paul Church, Hamble Road, Oadby,
LEICESTER
Tel: 01664 840661
Classical ballet school with tap and Theatre craft.

Maxine Phillips Dance Academy
LEICESTER
Tel: 0116 2773114

Midlands Academy of Dance & Drama
NOTTINGHAM
Tel: 0115 9110401

Mitton School of Dancing
LEICESTER
Tel: 0116 2109543

Morrison School of Dancing
NOTTINGHAM
Tel: 0115 9472537

Mrs J Godber
NOTTINGHAM
Tel: 0115 9608559

Newfoundpoole Neighbourhood Centre
LEICESTER
Tel: 0116 2367308

Nottingham Knights Dance Studio
NOTTINGHAM
Tel: 0115 9264169

Nottm Theatre Dance School
NOTTINGHAM
Tel: 0115 9117417

Ogando School of Dance
DERBYS
Tel: 01332 664916

Pat Barker Academy of Dance
LEICESTER
Tel: 01455 841166

Paterson Dance Society
LEICESTER
Tel: 0116 2991446

Patricia Eyre School of Dancing
NOTTINGHAM
Tel: 0115 9174576

Pirouette Academy of Dance
LEICESTER
Tel: 01455 285088

Premier School of Dancing
LEICESTER
Tel: 0116 2511084

Prima School of Dancing
NOTTINGHAM
Tel: 0115 9608559

R & M Knights Dance Studios
NOTTINGHAM
Tel: 0115 9501250

Ray Needham School of Dancing
NOTTINGHAM
Tel: 0115 8411779

Redhead-Scott School of Dancing
NOTTINGHAM
Tel: 0115 9228534

Rendevous For Dancing
DERBY
Tel: 01332 341925

Ripley Academy of Dance Ltd
DERBYS
Tel: 01773 745108

Ripley School of Dancing
DERBY
Tel: 01773 743324

Rochelle School of Dance
LEICESTER
Tel: 01455 636514

Rollo Academy of Dancing
NOTTINGHAM
Tel: 0115 9410928

Roy & Dorothy Moxon
DERBYS
Tel: 01283 542884

Royal Academy Of Dance
DERBYS
Tel: 01773 745108

Square Dance-On
NOTTINGHAM
Tel: 0115 9132387

Samantha Jane Loades
NOTTS
Tel: 0115 9323560

Shelby Dance Academy
LEICESTER
Tel: 01455 238003

Splitz Dance and Performing Arts Centre
DERBY
Tel: 01773 881072

Star Light Theatre School
LEICESTER
Tel: 0116 2355495

Starlight Academy of Dance
LEICESTER
Tel: 01455 848550

Steele Elliot School of Dancing
LEICESTER
Tel: 0116 2833964

Step In Time
NOTTINGHAM
Tel: 07980 815968

Stepping Out School of Dance
LEICESTER
Tel: 0116 2880804

Steps Schools of Theatre Dance
LEICESTER
Tel: 01455 282837

Studio's of Performing Arts
LEICESTER
Tel: 0116 2532696

Sundance Theatre School
LEICESTER
Tel: 0116 2766312

Susan Holman School Of Dance
LEICESTER
Tel: 0116 2374156

Sussenbach Stage School
LEICESTER
Tel: 0116 2236002

Tait-Stanley School of Dancing
NOTTINGHAM
Tel: 0115 9257891

The Ashbourne School of Dance
NOTTINGHAM
Tel: 0115 9735747

**The Burrows-Smith Academy
of Dancing**
BURTON ON TRENT
Tel: 01283 703773

The Lisa Maria School of Dancing
NOTTS
Tel: 0115 9641641

The Lorna Leighton School of Dancing
NOTTINGHAM
Tel: 0115 9651169

The Lutterworth Dance Studio
LEICESTER
Tel: 01455 557427

The Nickie Slater School of Dance
NOTTS
Tel: 01949 844642

The Patricia James School of Dance
NOTTINGHAM
Tel: 0115 9117740

The Rochelle School of Dance
LEICESTER
Tel: 01455 636514

The Sandra Taylor School of Dance
NOTTINGHAM
Tel: 0115 9816738

The Sarah Adamson School of Dance
NOTTS
Tel: 0115 9530397

The Stagecoach Theatre Arts Mansfield
29 Bryon Street, Mansfield, NOTTS
Tel: 01623 642061

The Vanessa Miller School of Dancing
Albert House, Derwent Street, Belper,
DERBYSHIRE
Tel: 01332 823309

Tozer Studios
NOTTINGHAM
Tel: 01636 815133

Tracy Quaife Theatre School
NOTTINGHAM
Tel: 0115 9414286

Trevonne Stage School
LEICESTER
Tel: 01664 566000

Vicky-Anne
Academy of Dance and Drama
LEICESTER
Tel: 07951 054140

Victoria Laidler
School of Dance
LEICESTER
Tel: 0116 2861141

Vanessa Millar
Albert House, Derwent St, Belper, DERBY
Tel: 01773 823 309

Vivienne Shelley Dance
DERBYS
Tel: 01538 723318

W Bates School of Dancing
BURTON-ON-TRENT
Tel: 01283 814471

Warrington School of Dancing
LEICESTER
Tel: 01455 553558

Wendy Morton Academy of
Dance & Model
LEICESTER
Tel: 01455 890578

Wigston School of Dance
LEICESTER
Tel: 0116 2810754

Dance International
NOTTINGHAM
Tel: 0115 958 5100

Dance Supplies
DERBYS
Tel: 01332 295968

Dance Supplies
DERBY
Tel: 01332 295968

Heart & Sole Dance Wear
131a Victoria Road, Netherfield, NOTTINGHAM
Tel: 0115 9118717
Web: www.heartnsole.co.uk

Let's Party Dancewear
91 High Street, Burton, DERBYS
Tel: 01283 511699
Web: www.letspartyletsdance.co.uk

Dance Wear Direct
LEICESTER
Tel: 0116 2354238

Dance World
BRISTOL
Tel: 0117 9537941

Dance-Rite
NOTTS
Tel: 0115 9305580

Dancewear Direct
LEICESTER
Tel: 0116 2354238

Dancia International
NOTTINGHAM
Tel: 0115 9585100

David Young Knitting
NOTTS
Tel: 01773 714333

Elite Dance Supplies
BURTON ON TRENT
Tel: 01283 701452

Etoile Dancewear Ltd
DERBY
Tel: 01332 371482

Etoile Dancewear Ltd
DERBY
Tel: 01332 371482

Hardings Dancewear
NOTTINGHAM
Tel: 0115 9418767

Lets Party Dancewear
DERBYSHIRE
Tel: 01283 511699

Only Joking
DERBY
Tel: 01332 295968

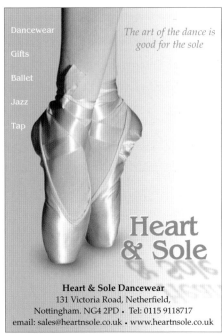

1st Act Entertainments
LEICESTER
Tel: 0116 2415265

1st Choice Entertainments
LEICESTER
Tel: 0116 2880030

1st Sounds
LEICESTER
Tel: 0116 2490577

A A & B Reflections Discos
NOTTINGHAM
Tel: 0115 9615626

Ace Disco
LEICESTER
Tel: 0116 2419108

Ace of Hearts Roadshow
LEICESTER
Tel: 0116 2822205

Advance Discos & Karaoke
NOTTINGHAM
Tel: 0115 8479759

Andy's Twilight Sound Disco
LEICESTER
Tel: 01509 235183
AS Disco
LEICESTER
Tel: 0116 2228196

Ask Adrian Entertainments
LEICESTER
Tel: 0116 2784159

Atlanta Disco
LEICESTER
Tel: 01530 839176

Atmosphere Inc
DERBY
Tel: 01332 346641

Atomic Sounds Disco
DERBY
Tel: 01283 215563

Bassline
Mobile Disco
LEICESTER
Tel: 07796 081296

Ben's Mobile Discos
LEICS
Tel: 07736 320803
Web: www.bensmobilediscos.com

Blaze Disco
DERBYS
Tel: 08000 858 456

Cream Entertainments Ltd
LEICESTER
Tel: 0116 2861720

Dancemaster
Mobile Disco
LEICESTER
Tel: 01664 851578
Web: www.dancemasterdisco.co.uk

Darren Jackson
LEICS
Tel: 01530 564098

Dave Dee
STOKE-ON-TRENT
Tel: 08456 444161

Dave Hawke Disco
LEICESTER
Tel: 01858 466193

Disco 2000
DERBYS
Tel: 07973 749049

Disco Ed
LEICESTER
Tel: 0116 2596838

DJ Mobile Disco
DERBYS
Tel: 01332 875759

Double Disc
LEICS
Tel: 0800 0186347
Web: www.double-disc.co.uk

Double K Disco
DERBYS
Tel: 01335 370159

Electric Dreams Entertainment
LEICESTER
Tel: 0116 2784216

Empire DJs
LEICESTER
Tel: 0116 2250498
Web: www.empire-djs.co.uk

Enigma Entertainments
LEICESTER
Tel: 07818 296913

Entertainments by Pogo
NOTTINGHAM
Tel: 0115 9611190

Future Disco
LEICESTER
Tel: 0116 2356279

High Time Disco
LEICESTER
Tel: 0116 2848951

Hotshots
DERBYS
Tel: 01332 605584

Infextious
DERBYS
Tel: 0800 0287156

JJ's Music Machine & Light Disco
NOTTINGHAM
Tel: 0115 9309543

J's Disco Services
LEICESTER
Tel: 0116 2248831

K.C Disco
DERBYS
Tel: 01889 536621

Kidz Discos
DERBYS
Tel: 01283 530551

Kings Discos
LEICESTER
Tel: 01858 440523

Melissa's Entertainments & Royale Disco
LEICESTER
Tel: 01530 244213

Millenium Roadshows
DERBY
Tel: 01332 369329

Mitre Entertainers
DERBY
Tel: 07876 652231

Mitre Entertainments
LEICESTER
Tel: 07876 652231

MR A M Lenton
DERBYS
Tel: 01283 540373

Multi-Mix Music
DERBYSHIRE
Tel: 07957 983724

Music Box Disco
LEICESTER
Tel: 0116 2600049

Musicmix Mobile Disco
LEICESTER
Tel: 0116 2108321

Mystic Warrior Sound Inc
LEICESTER
Tel: 0116 2607416

Nightair
NOTTINGHAM
Tel: 0800 389 6399

NPS Discotheques
NOTTS
Tel: 01773 510642

Pandemonium International Discotheque
NOTTINGHAM
Tel: 0115 9222959

Phoenix Discotheque
NOTTINGHAM
Tel: 0115 9770051

Planet Disco
NOTTINGHAM
Tel: 0115 8497661

Porky's Digital Mobile Discotheque
DERBY
Tel: 01332 668978

Pure Gold Entertainment
LEICESTER
Tel: 01509 550017
Web: www.pure-entertainment.150m.com

Rainbow Entertainments
DERBYS
Tel: 07979 775302

Roadblock Mobile Disco
LEICESTER
Tel: 0116 2403798

Sam Jam
NOTTS
Tel: 01949 851223

Sam's Party & Disco-Karaoke
DERBYS
Tel: 01283 213665

Sapphire Roadshow
NOTTINGHAM
Tel: 0115 9846005

Seti Discos
LEICESTER
Tel: 07788 595158

Shaun Alan Entertainments
LEICESTER
Tel: 0116 2877051
Web: www.djshaunalan.co.uk

Solid Gold Disco
LEICESTER
Tel: 01455 238690

Sonic Sound Roadshow
DERBYS
Tel: 01773 826709

Soul Sauce Mobile Discos
NOTTINGHAM
Tel: 0115 9899567

Sound City Disco
LEICESTER
Tel: 01530 812407

Sound Machine Roadshow
LEICESTER
Tel: 01509 556705
Sound Sensation
DERBY
Tel: 07944 451779

Sounds Wright Disco
DERBY
Tel: 01332 369522

Spectrum Disco & Karaoke
LEICESTER
Tel: 01455 251920

ST Roadshow
LEICESTER
Tel: 0116 2246285

Stewards Mobile Disco
LEICESTER
Tel: 0116 2919154

Storm Light and Sound
NOTTS
Tel: 0949 878277

Discos

Strictly Dance
NOTTINGHAM
Tel: 0115 9618375

Super Sounds
DERBYS
Tel: 07793 400953

Super Star Sound & Entertainment
LEICESTER
Tel: 01509 214343

Systems Roadshow
LEICESTER
Tel: 01509 216379

Tall Order Roadshow
DERBYS
Tel: 01332 753508

Tech Noir
DERBYS
Tel: 01283 215876

The Music Men
LEICESTER
Tel: 01530 81092

U.K Discotheques
NOTTS
Tel: 0115 9224390

Unit 4 Roadshow
DERBY
Tel: 01332 672780

Wall of Sound
NOTTINGHAM
Tel: 0115 9385374

Wheels of Steel Mobile Disco
LEICESTER
Tel: 0116 2217263

**Whittaker's Lunch Packs
Revival Discos**
DERBYS
Tel: 01283 516387

Wobblers International
NOTTINGHAM
Tel: 0115 9231665

Doctors

NHS Direct
NOTTINGHAM
Tel: 0845 4647

Dolls & Dolls Houses

Dollshouse Cottage Workshop
NOTTINGHAM
Tel: 0115 9465059

Dolly Dolittle's
LEICESTER
Tel: 01858 466262

M J News & Dolls Houses
NOTTINGHAM
Email: mickjohal@ntlworld.com
Web: www.ntlworld.com

Matilda's Miniatures
PETERBOROUGH
Tel: 01778 424222

The Dolly Lodge
NORTHAMPTON
Tel: 01604 812852

The English Rose Dolls House
DERBY
Tel: 01332 290802
Web: www.theenglishrosedollshouse.co.uk

The Miniature Cellar

*Yesterdays Style Todays - Quality
- Tomorrows Heirlooms*

Contact John & Linda for help & advice

27 Radcliffe Gate, Mansfield,
Notts. NG18 2JA
Tel: 01623 623520

email: enquiries@theminiaturecellar.co.uk
web: www.theminiaturecellar.co.uk

The Miniture Cellar
27 Ratcliffe Gate, Mansfield, NOTTS
Tel: 01623 623520
Email: enquiries@theminiturecellar.co.uk
Web: www.theminiturecellar.co.uk
Dolls houses, furniture and accessories.

Wood 'n' Wotnots
NOTTINGHAM
Tel: 0115 9430567

Doll and Bear Hospital (Midlands)
STAFFORD
Tel: 01785 241 726

Nottingham Teddy Bear Hospital
230 Wigman Road, Bilborough, NOTTINGHAM
Tel: 0115 8778985

Birth Matters
BELPER
Tel: 01773 826055
Email: diane@vizion.fsnet.co.uk
Web: www.vizion.fsnet.co.uk
See main advert on page 13

British Doulas
49 Harrington Gardens, London
Tel: 020 7244 6053
Web: www.britishdoulas.co.uk
Call to find your local Doula, Nanny, Maternity Nurse and Mothers Help. Cover the whole Uk.

First Breath Doulas
266 Wyggeston Street, Burton On Trent,
DERBYS
Tel: 01283 535818
Web: www.firstbreathdoulas.co.uk
Compassionate birth support at home or hospital throughout the Midlands.

Taylor Maid
9 Sandale Close, Gamston,
NOTTINGHAM
Tel: 0115 9817175
Email: tracy @ taylormaiddoulas.co.uk
Help in the home for mums with newborn babies.

Ashworth Studio
Dance/Drama
NOTTINGHAM
Tel: 0115 9312573

Barbara Musk
DERBY
Tel: 01283 517094

Capital Arts Children Choir
LEICESTER
Tel: 0116 2672035

Dazzle Stage Scholl
NOTTINGHAM
Tel: 0771 244734

Guillain School of Theatre
LEICESTER
Tel: 0116 2215684

Helen O'Grady
NOTTINGHAM
Tel: 0115 8545460

Hinckley Speech &
Drama Studio
6 Trafford Road, Hinckley,
LEICESTER
Tel: 01455 230317
Email: info@hsds.biz
Web: www.hsds.biz
Have fun while learning communication
skills for life-age 4 upwards.

Stage Coach
Theatre Arts
DERBYS
Tel: 01332 512555

Stage Coach
Theatre Arts
LEICESTER
Tel: 01664 424744

Stage Coach
Theatre Arts
NOTTINGHAM
Tel: 0115 9258250

Kumon: an education for life

Whatever your child wants to achieve in life, a solid foundation in maths and English is essential.

With the year-round Kumon programmes, children develop confidence, discipline and study skills that last them a lifetime.

Contact your local Instructor

Allestree	01773 825291
Ashby-de-la-Zouch	01283 538391
Beeston	0115 945 9941
Blaby	0116 272 0371
Chesterfield	01246 275159
Derby, Oakwood	01158 499290
Derby	01332 835833
Leicester, Glenfield	0116 281 2149
Leicester, Rushey Mead	0116 221 9792
Leicester, Stoney Gate	0116 221 9538
Long Eaton	0115 972 5185
Loughborough	01530 242814
Market Harborough	0116 272 0371
Newark	01636 814217
Sherwood	0115 845 0330
Southwell	01623 882844
Stapleford	01332 862357
Wollaton Vale	0115 972 5185

0800 854 714
www.kumon.co.uk
Quote ref: 4321

KUMON

For almost 50 years, children around the world have benefited from studying the Kumon maths and native language programmes. 45,000 children of all ages and abilities are currently enrolled at study centres throughout the UK. There is a one-off enrolment fee of £15, and monthly tuition fees are only £41 per subject, per child.

Education

54

Professional Tutoring
in Reading, Spelling, English
& Maths at

KipMcGrath
EDUCATION
CENTRES

*The Highest quality tuition available
for 6 - 16 year olds.
Provided by qualified, experienced teachers.*

FREE ASSESSMENT
Call Jean Willgoose Now on: 0115 9280202
185 Bramcote Lane, Wollaton, NG8 2QL
Admin@kmecwollaton.force9.co.uk
www.kipmcgrath.com

Crystal Clear Learning
DERBYSHIRE
Tel: 0800 587 8823

Kip McGrath
DERBY
Tel: 01332 670817

Kip McGrath Education Centre
185 Bramcote Lane, Wollaton, NOTTS
Tel: 0115 9280202
*Kip McGrath education centre, Wollaton.
Professional tutoring for children.*

Kumon Educational
Foxhall Business Centre, Foxhall Road,
NOTTINGHAM
Tel: 0800 854714
Web: www.kumon.co.uk

Number Works Beeston
25 Wollaton Road, Beeston,
NOTTINGHAM
Tel: 0115 9252565
Web: www.numberworks.com

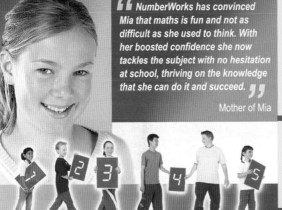

Education

Private Tutors Nottingham
8 Highcroft Drive, NOTTINGHAM
Tel: 0115 928 6646
Web: www.private-tutors-nottingham.co.uk
*Private Tutorials 5-18 years. All subjects
covered including language, literacy and
numeracy.*

The Student Support Centre
Tel: 0800 13 22 77

Entertainers

1st Ask Scott Thompson
LEICS
Tel: 01530 838012

1st Barn Dances
NOTTS
Tel: 01509 673867

A Magical Adventure Theatre
NOTTINGHAM
Tel: 0115 9332882

Abracadabra
NOTTS
Tel: 01159 261543

Abracadabra
Childrens Entertainments
LEICESTER
Tel: 0116 2331008

Andrew De Burgh
LEICESTER
Tel: 01530 834743

Arty Party Face Painting
NOTTINGHAM
Tel: 0115 9206390

Auntie Happy
NOTTINGHAM
Tel: 0115 9225499

Barrie Perkins
NOTTINGHAM
Tel: 0115 9283080

Barry Kay
NOTTINGHAM
Tel: 0115 9147314

Bolt From The Blue
LEICESTER
Tel: 07748 943145
Email: boltfromtheblue@msn.com

Boo Boo The Clown
WARWICKSHIRE
Tel: 0800 371266

Boo-Boo The Clown
LEICESTER
Tel: 01530 413998
Email: avidcooper@ashby7777.
fsbusiness.co.uk

Bubbles The Clown
DERBYS
Tel: 01332 669131

Children's & Corporate Entertainments
COVENTRY
Tel: 024 76450683

Chris Gillingam Entertainment &
Fun Hire
LEICESTER
Tel: 01530 452044
Web: www.funhire.co.uk

Chuckle Chops & Chums
LEICESTER
Tel: 01530 457786
Web: www.chucklechops.co.uk

Cliff Carlton and Carlo the Clown
DERBYS
Tel: 01773 856796

Clown Zozo
DERBYS
Tel: 01159 300070

Discotainment
WESTERN SUBEDGE
Tel: 0800 0854034

Doodles Professional Face Painting
NOTTINGHAM
Tel: 0115 8400529

Fantastic Fun Faces
LEICESTER
Tel: 0116 2340671

Fizzy The Fairy Clown
NOTTINGHAM
Tel: 0115 953 2587

Flip & Flop Clowns
LEICESTER
Tel: 01530 224369

FLO-The Children's Entertainer
LEICESTER
Tel: 01283 552283

Freddie Magical Entertainer
NOTTINGHAM
Tel: 0115 9614551

Funtasia
LEICESTER
Tel: 01455 550949

Girls Beauty Parties
NOTTINGHAM
Tel: 0115 975 7500

Gizzo's Entertainments
LEICESTER
Tel: 0116 2415265

Glenn Bonnar Child Magic
LEICESTER
Tel: 01455 284743

Glitzy Girls Parties
19 Lincoln Drive, Mansfield, NOTTS
Tel: 01623 633963
Web: www.glitzygirls.co.uk

Helen Magill HND,ITEC
NOTTINGHAM
Tel: 0115 9639037

J.J.Max & Tilly Minth The Clown
DERBYS
Tel: 01283 219081

Jack in the Box
50 Westwick Road, NOTTINGHAM
Tel: 0115 9138431
Fully insured bouncy castles for party hire, fetes and school.

Jesters Entertainment
LEICESTER
Tel: 0116 2402796
Email: rileyjesters@aol.com

Jolly Face Painting
NOTTINGHAM
Tel: 0115 950 4411

Jolly Jingles Funtime
45 Co-operative Street, Long Eaton, NOTTINGHAM
Tel: 0845 0090848
Email: clown@jollyjingles.co.uk
Web: www.jollyjingles.co.uk

Jolly's Face Painting
NOTTINGHAM
Tel: 0115 9504411

Karl The Magician
LEICESTER
Tel: 01455 841398

Katz Entertainment
LEICESTER
Tel: 0116 2605381

Kids 'Discotainment' Parties
LEICESTER
Tel: 0800 0854034

Lollipops The Clown
LEICESTER
Tel: 0116 2415176

Magic Bryan
NOTTINGHAM
Tel: 0115 9209025

Magical Enteatinment
NOTTINGHAM
Tel: 0115 970 8535

Mark Garside
NOTTINGHAM
Tel: 0115 9708535

Maxine Fairey
LEICESTER

Monster Massive
NOTTINGHAM
Tel: 0845 4561597
Email: monstermassive@
monstermassive.co.uk
Web: www.monstermassive.co.uk

Mr & Mrs Custard
LEICESTER
Tel: 01536 771881
Web: www.mrcustard.com

Mr Potato By Eddie Nunan
LEICESTER
Tel: 01827 873503

Mr. Oddsocks
LEICESTER
Tel: 024 76375832

Pandora
NOTTINGHAM
Tel: 0115 9232526

**Pandors and Performing/
Community Arts**
NOTTINGHAM
Tel: 0115 923 2526

Peter Presto
NOTTINGHAM
Tel: 0115 9816407

Pete's Funny Farm
NOTTINGHAM
Tel: 0115 9816690/07960 352147

Pogo The Clown
NOTTINGHAM
Tel: 0115 9611190
Web: www.pogoclown.com

Popsy The Clown
LEICESTER
Tel: 0116 2303068

Ray Raymond
NOTTINGAM
Tel: 0115 9250442

Revel Devil Parties
Tel: 0115 915 2726
Web: www.nottingham.gov.uk/leisurecentres

Richard Fawkes
LOUGHBOROUGH
Tel: 07774 171070

Robin Hood Hire
Tel: 0115 966 5522
Web: www.robibhoodhire.co.uk

Rogers Kirkby Table Magic
NOTTINGHAM
Tel: 0115 8410350
Web: www.rogerkirkbymagician.co.uk

Silisosige Entertainments
LEICESTER
Tel: 0808 1080500

Smudgie The Clown
LEICESTER
Tel: 01455 250094

Squiggles, Teapot & Friends
LEICESTER
Tel: 01455 286292

Stretton 2000
LEICESTER
Tel: 0116 2592900

Sylvester The Jester
LEICESTER
Tel: 0116 2545876

Tom Turnip The Clown
LEICESTER
Tel: 0116 2848478

Will Gray Magician
LEICESTER
Tel: 01530 457465

William's World of Fun
LEICESTER
Tel: 0116 2832318

Contraception & Sexual Health Service
NOTTINGHAM
Tel: 0115 9509151

Family Planning Association
LONDON
Tel: 0845 3101334

Fancy Dress

Balloon & Party Ideas
DERBYS
Tel: 0115 9242345

Balloonatics
LEICESTER
Tel: 01455 233444

Cabaret Costumes
LEICESTER
Tel: 0116 2511105
Web: www.costumehire.tv

Costume Corner
LEICESTER
Tel: 0116 2541513

Costume Hire
LEICESTER
Tel: 0116 2538949
Web: www.costumehire.co.uk

Fancy Dress @ Party Party
NOTTINGHAM
Tel: 0115 9583548

Fancy Dress Hire
LEICESTER
Tel: 0116 2880030

Fantasia
LEICESTER
Tel: 01536 201401

Fantasy Dress Hire
LEICESTER
Tel: 01530 413998

Harlequin Hire
LEICESTER
Tel: 0116 2855141

Jolly Jesters Fancy Dress
DERBYS
Tel: 01773 609616

Little Theatre Costumes Hire
LEICESTER
Tel: 0116 2540472
Web: www.thelittletheatre.net

Masquerade Fancy Dress
LEICS
Tel: 01509 261160

Oodles
NOTTS
Tel: 01623 6294911

Paper Tiger
LEICESTER
Tel: 0116 2519345

Sukies Fancy Dress & Costume Hire
PETERBOROUGH
Tel: 01780 754829

The Golden Cage
NOTTINGHAM
Tel: 0115 9411600

The Magic Touch
LEICESTER
Tel: 01858 468477

Victoria Costumes
NOTTINGHAM
Tel: 0115 9110051
Web: www.victoriacostumes.co.uk

Farms

Ferry Farm Country Park
NOTTINGHAM
Tel: 0115 9664512
Web: www.ferryfarm.co.uk

Gorse Hill City Farm
LEICESTER
Tel: 0116 2537582

Manor Farm Animal Centre
Manor Farm, Castle Hill, East Leake,
Loughborough, LEICESTER
Tel: 01509 852525

Sherwood Forest Farm Park
Lamb Pen Farm Park, Edwinstowe,
NR MANSFIELD, Notts
Tel: 01623 823558
Web: www.sherwoodforestfarmpark.co.uk
Great day out for parents and children.

The Whitepost Modern Farm
Mansfield Road, Farnsfield,
NOTTINGHAM
Tel: 01623 882977

Twinlakes Park
Melton Spinney Road,
Melton Mowbray,
LEICESTER
Tel: 01664 567777

White Post Farm Centre
Mansfield Road, Farnsfield, NOTTS
Tel: 01623 882977
Web: www.whitepostfarmcentre.co.uk
Great day out for all the family.
Make friends with over 3,000 animals.
Suitable for children 1-100!

Fatherhood

Fathers Direct
Web: www.fathersdirect.com

The Children Need Fathers Organisation
Tel: 0870 794 0075

Feng-Shui

Creative Space
NOTTINGHAM
Tel: 0115 9857399

Elemental Feng Shui
NOTTS
Tel: 01949 831759
Web: www.elementalfengshui.co.uk

Feng Shui For Living
DERBY
Tel: 01773 833228

Lindsay Nash MCH RSHom
LONDON
Tel: 0115 9692190

Hampton Dean
5 Castle Bridge Office Village,
Castle Marina, NOTTINGHAM
Tel: 0115 9886997
Email: steve.collyer@hamptondean.co.uk
Web: www.hamptondean.co.uk
Independant Financial advisers - for the financial protection for you and your family.

First Aid Training

"Don't wait 'til it's too late, Be-Prepared"
Beginner & refresher First Aid courses for the workplace & home
We just don't show you How
We help you understand Why

10 Lulworth Close,
West Bridgford,
Nottingham. NG2 7UB
Tel: 0115 9143 999
parenting@be-prepared.co.uk
www.be-prepared.co.uk

Be Prepared
First Aid Training

Be-Prepared
10 Lulworth Close, West Bridgford,
NOTTINGHAM
Tel: 0115 9143999
First Aid training and supplies.
HSE approved courses including child carers and parents.

Bristish Red Cross
NOTTINGHAM
Tel: 0115 9789222
Web: www.redcross.org.uk

First Responder Ltd
LEICESTER
Tel: 0116 2832700

Medic 112
NORTHAMPTON
Tel: 0800 0198029

Mobile First Aid Training
LINCS
Tel: 01205 270089

Olympic Training
NOTTINGHAM
Tel: 0115 9784035

St John Ambulance
NOTTINGHAM
Tel: 0115 9784625

Star Care Services
NOTTINGHAM
Tel: 0115 9382391

Football

Soccerama
DERBY
Tel: 01332 349193

The Coerver Coaching Method
LEICESTER
Tel: 07881 805725

Vida Short Sided Soccer Ltd
NOTTINGHAM
Tel: 0115 9295442/9295888

Youth Soccer
NOTTINGHAM
Tel: 0115 955 2830
Email: patman@youthsoccer.co.uk
Web: www.youthsoccer.co.uk

Fostering

Fostering Service
NOTTS
Tel: 01636 687382

"*Don't wait 'til it's too late,*

Be + Prepared"

First Aid Training

Accidents and injuries can occur at any time and often have cause for alarm especially when childfren are involved. When it happens it is important that one knows how to deal with an injury safely, in a clear manner, providing reassurance to the person and assisting a speedy recovery. Learning First Aid may save the life of one's family, friends, loved ones or workmates. Be-Prepared have a range of training courses to suit every person. Some of the area covered are:

- How and why accidents occur
- Coping with accidents
- Resuscitation
- Burns and scalds
- Miscellaneous injuries
- Eye injuries / irritation
- Common illness
- Infantile convulsions
- Asthma

- Accident prevention & safety
- The unconscious child
- Control of bleeding
- Treatment of shock
- Poisoning
- Epileptic fit
- Head injuries
- Choking
- Fractures

We take pride in our training as our aim is customer care and satisfaction. Our mission statement is:

"We just don't show you How
We help you understand Why"

We give personal attention to each person so that you develop a clear understanding of how to deal with an injury. We offer complete flexibility as the training times and course contents are based to suit your needs.

Any non medical injury topic that is unique to you is included free within the course. We offer free on-going confidence building support to you after the end of the course.

Our certificated courses lead to nationally recognised qualifications and the training is given to you by experienced, qualified and professional Trainers.

Some of the benefits to you that we offer are:-

We provide training at places to suit you, such as in the comfort of your living room, as we understand that it is not always possible to travel to training courses. This also saves you travelling time and expense.

For further information, telephone:
Be-Prepared on 0115 9143 999
or email: parenting@be-prepared.co.uk

Dignity Fairtrade
NOTTINGHAM
Tel: 07790 329 685

Evolution
42 Oxford Street, Ripley
DERBYS
Tel: 01773 744553
Web: www.designerclothes4kids.co.uk
Large selection of designer wear, including shoes, gifts and christening wear.

Hot-hands
13 Malvern Road, West Bridgford
NOTTINGHAM
Tel: 0115 8781805
Web: www.hot-hands.co.uk
Your child's hands or foot prints individually portrayed on a uniquely designed and coloured canvas" recording their little size forever." Colours selected to suit home interior. Prices start from £29.00

Jellyrolls
25 Francis Street, LEICESTER
Tel: 0116 2704277

Life Casting Nottingham
10 Powtrell Place, Ilkeston
NOTTINGHAM
Tel: 0115 9306772
Web: www.life-casting-uk.co.uk

Proud 2b Maternity Boutique
5 Loseby Lane, LEICESTER
Tel: 0116 2621127
Maternity wear and accessories.

Second Skin
40 Barrow Road, Quorn, Loughborough
LEICS
Tel: 01509 557393
Web: www.secondskin.uk.net

Swells Maternity Wear
Newark Road, Alverton, NOTTS
Tel: 01949 850263
Web: www.swells.co.uk

Swells Maternity Wear
Drury Walk, Broadmarsh Centre,
NOTTINGHAM

Tel: 0115 9470408
Web: www.swells.co.uk
Established 16 years ago, Swells offers 6 different European fashion collections for all tastes and occasions. Our staff are fully trained to fit the 4 pre-natal and nursing bra ranges and offer a high level of personal service advice when needed.

Whizzy Wheels
69 Queens Road, Clarendon Park,
LEICESTER
Tel: 0116 2702888
Email: info@whizzywheels.co.uk
Web: www.whizzywheels.co.uk
Former mid-wife and neo-natal nurse owner. Bespoke service tailored to customer requirements. Free impartial advice.

Denby Pottery Visitor Centre
on B6179, off A38, 2 miles south of Ripley,
Denby, DERBYS
Tel: 01773 740700
Lot's of activities & entertainment, for children, during school holidays.

Gyms for Children

Jumping Beans Fitkid Club
The Willows, Melton Mowbray
LEICESTER
Tel: 07790 007713

Angels
ASHBY DE LA ZOUCH
Tel: 01530 412050

Branston Golf & Country Club
Burton Road, Branston,
BURTON UPON TRENT, Staffs
Tel: 01283 512211

Champneys Spring Health Resort
MEASHAM
Tel: 01530 273873

David Lloyd Leisure
NOTTINGHAM
Tel: 0115 9825555

David Lloyd Leisure
NOTTINGHAM
Tel: 0115 9007001

David Lloyd Leisure
DERBY
Tel: 01332 821306
Email: www.davidlloydleisure.co.uk

Derbyshire Pilates
DERBYS
Tel: 01332 557980

Eden Hall Day Spa
NEWARK
Tel: 01636 525 555

Eden Ladies Health and Fitness
LEICESTER
Tel: 0116 2778899

Hoar Cross Hall Health Spa Resort,
Hoar Cross
Tel: 01283 575671

Holmes Place
NOTTINGHAM
Tel: 0115 9884747

Living Well
LEICESTER
Tel: 0116 2046500

Roko Health Club
NOTTINGHAM
Tel: 0115 9827799

Tai Chi Temple
LEICESTER
Tel: 0116 255 7055

Aloe-2-U
LEICESTER
Tel: 0116 2593976

Ceres
NOTTINGHAM
Tel: 01773 769540

Corsons Health Food & Home Brew
NOTTINGHAM
Tel: 0115 9814080

Currant Affairs
LEICESTER
Tel: 0116 2510887

Elf Foods
LEICESTER
Tel: 01509 212424

Farm Gate Products
LEICESTER
Tel: 0116 2713086

General Nutrition Centres
NOTTINGHAM
Tel: HO 01283 560078

General Nutrition Centres
NUNEATON, WARWIICKSHIRE
Tel: 0116 2624859

Health & Whole Foods
LEICESTER
Tel: 0116 2671677

Healthwise
NOTTINGHAM
Tel: 0115 9625487

Healthy Living
LEICESTER
Tel: 0116 2539097

Healthyfoodstore.co.uk
LEICESTER
Tel: 0116 2213130

Holland & Barratt
NOTTINGHAM
Tel: 0115 9447626

Holland & Barrett
LEICESTER
Tel: 01455 251258

Hongtu Health Foods Ltd
LEICESTER
Tel: 01509 268934

Julian Graves Ltd
NOTTINGHAM
Tel: 01636 610973
Fax: 1636

Julian Graves Ltd
LEICESTER
Tel: 01664 482848

Kirkgate Healthfoods
NOTTS
Tel: 01636 612230

Leicester Wholefood Co-op
LEICESTER
Tel: 0116 2512525

Little London Health Stores
4 Kings Walk, NOTTINGHAM
Tel: 0115 9472854
Establised over 100 years-knowledgeable staff-wide range of vitamins, herbs, aromatherapy oils for every aspect of life.

Natural Choice
LEICESTER
Tel: 01455 635254

Natural Food Co
NOTTINGHAM
Tel: 0115 9559914

Natural Healthcare
LEICESTER
Tel: 01530 831166

Naturally Health
LEICESTER
Tel: 01530 243225

Natures Dispensary
LEICESTER
Tel: 01572 771231

Rosemarys Health Foods
WOLVERHAMPTON
Tel: 0115 9505072

Screaming Carrot Vegetarian Bakery
NOTTINGHAM
Tel: 0115 9103013

The Health Store
LEICESTER
Tel: 0116 2889424

The Health Store at Sunflower
DERBYS
Tel: 0115 9304750

Thorpes Health Food
LEICESTER
Tel: 01664 567727

West Point Pharmacy
NOTTINGHAM
Tel: 0115 9736620

Holidays

Aviemore Highland Resort
HIGHLANDS
Tel: 0870 1244124
Web: www.aviemorehighlandresort.com

Babinton House
SOMERSET
Tel: 01373 812266

Center Parcs
Tel: 08708 408435
Web: www.centerparcs.com

Classic Cottages
Tel: 01326 555555

Clebe House Luxury Cottages
Tel: 01288 381272

Coast & Country Cottages
Tel: 01548 843773
Web: www.coastandcountry.co.uk

Coombe Mill
CORNWALL
Tel: 01208 950344
Web: www.coombemill.com

Coppid Beach Hotel
BERKSHIRE
Tel: 01344 303333
Web: www.coppidbeach.com

Hannafore Point Hotel
CORNWALL
Tel: 01503 263273
Web: www.hannaforepointhotel.com

Fowley Hall
CORNWALL
Tel: 01726 833866
Web: www.luxuryfamilhollidays.com

Higher Lank Farm
CORNWALL
Tel: 01208 850716

Individual France
Tel: 08700 780185

Moonfleet Manor
DORSET
Tel: 01305 786948
Web: www.luxuryfamilyholidays.com

Organic Holidays
Tel: 01943 970791
Email: lindamoss@organicholidays.com
Web: www.organicholidays.com

Polurriabn Hotel
CORNWALL
Tel: 01326 240421
Web: www.polurotel@aol.com

Priory Bay
ISLE OF WIGHT
Tel: 0870 444 8890
Web: www.redfunnelholidays.co.uk

Sands Resort Hotel
CORNWALL
Tel: 01637 872 864
Web: www.sandsresort.co.uk

Stately Holiday Homes
Tel: 01638 674749

The Ickworth
SUFFOLK
Tel: 01284 735350
Web: www.luxuryfamilyholidays.com

The Knoll House
STUDLAND BAY
Tel: 01929 450450
Web: www.knollhouse.co.uk

PROTECT YOUR CHILD

Don't let your children suffer from unbearable
heat & damaging UV rays this summer

Tinting your vehicle will cut 99% of the suns harmful UV rays & block out up to 73% of unwanted heat.

(Tinting also stops flying pieces of glass should the vehicle be involved in an accident, provides added safety to passengers)

Choose from a range of quality tints in varying shades.

Prices start from £195 + VAT

Collection and delivery servcie or courtesy car (please call for availability)

Please call for further information

0116 279 3113

(also available domestic/commercial window film services)

PROTECT YOUR CHILD

Don't let your children suffer from unbearable Heat & damaging UV rays this summer

BENEFITS OF CAR TINTING

SECURITY: Pro-tint use film which laminates your windows making it harder to break through.

SAFETY: Passengers are protected from flying glass in the event of an accident.

COOLING: Pro-tint films reflect heat, keeping your car cooler.

SKIN DISORDERS: All the films used block 99% of UV Light

ECONOMY: The cooler your car the less the air-conditioning is needed

PRIVACY: With the rear of your car darkened, thieves have less chance of spotting valuables.

Pro-tint House, Unit 4, Kingsley Business Park,
New Road, Kibworth, Leicester LE8 0LE
Telephone 0116 2793113 . Fax 0116 279 3224
www.pro-tint.co.uk . Email sales@pro-tint.co.uk

The Samling
LAKE WINDERMERE
Tel: 01539 431922

Watergate Bay Hotel
CORNWALL
Tel: 01637 860543
Web: www.watergatebay.co.uk

Woolacombe Bay
NORTH DEVON
Tel: 01272 870 388
Web: www.woolacombe-bay-hotel.co.uk

Woolacombe Bay Holiday Park
NORTH DEVON
Tel: 01272 870 343
Web: www.woolacombe.com

Wooley Grange
WILTSHIRE
Tel: 01255 864705
Web: www.luxuryfamilyholidays.com

Yew Tree Farm
CUMBRIA
Tel: 01539 411433
Web: www.yewtree-farm.com

Holiday Internet Sites

www.babiestravellite.com

www.babygoes2.com

www.takethefamily.com

www.tinytravellers.net

Homeopathy

Alliance of Registered Homoeopaths
CORBY
Tel: 01536 744520

Andrew Meyer
LEICESTER
Tel: 01455 282940

Belper Natural Health Centre
Belper, DERBYS
Tel: 01773 820220

Derby Homeopathic Surgery
DERBY
Tel: 01332 726473

Desai Shilpa
LEICESTER
Tel: 07739 102913

East Gate Complimentary Health
LEICESTER
Tel: 0116 2511647

Eastgate Complementary Health Centre
19 Humberstone Road, LEICESTER
Tel: 0116 2511647
Pre-natal and post-natal care. Special infant & childrens clinic. Establised since 1996. Fully qualified and insured.

Homepathy
NOTTINGHAM
Tel: 0115 979 9550

Jo Hale
DERBY
Tel: 01332 299133

Kim Campion
LEICESTER
Tel: 0116 2107680

Lucy Shaw
Tofts Farm Oak House, Farmer Street,
Bradmore, NOTTINGHAM
Tel: 0115 9825353

Lynch Joseph
LEICESTER
Tel: 0116 2511647

M.D. Pook
The Ropewalk, NOTTINGHAM
Tel: 0115 9472263

Marie Lenage LCH Homoeopath
LEICESTER
Tel: 01509 230200

Nottingham Natural Health Centre For Babies and Children
NOTTINGHAM
Tel: 0115 9608855

Orchard Medical Practice
LEICESTER
Tel: 01455 282940

Society of Homeopathy
NORTHAMPTON
Tel: 0845 4506611

The Society of Homoepaths
NORTHANTS
Tel: 01604 817890

Valerie Kemp MHMA LCPH
LEICESTER
Tel: 0116 2220739

Vicki Hill
Gedling, NOTTINGHAM
Tel: 0115 987 7103

Derby City General Hospital
Uttoxeter Road, DERBY
Tel: 01332 340131

Derbyshire Royal Infimary
London Road, DERBY
Tel: 01332 347141

Glenfield Hospital NHS Trust
Groby Road, Glenfield LEICESTER
Tel: 0116 2871471

Leicester General Hospital
Gwendolen Road, LEICESTER
Tel: 0116 2490490

Nottingham City Hospital N.H.S Trust
Hucknall Road, Sherwood NOTTINGHAM
Tel: 0115 9691169

Queen's Medical Centre
Derby Road, NOTTINGHAM
Tel: 0115 9249924

Hospitals Private

BMI The Park Hospital
Sherwood Lodge Drive, Burntstump
Country Park, Arnold, NOTTINGHAM
Tel: 0115 9670670

Bupa Hospital Leicester
Gartree Road, Oadby, LEICESTER
Tel: 0116 2653691

Bupa Hospital Little Aston
Little Aston Hall Drive, LITTLE ASTON
Tel: 0121 353 2444

Bupa Wellness Centre
1st Floor, Unit K, Phoenix Park West,
Millenium Way West, NOTTINGHAM
Tel: 0845 6014914
Web: www.bupa.co.uk

Nuffield Hospital-Derby
Rykneld Road, Littleover, DERBYS
Tel: 01332 517891

Nuffield Hospital-Leicester
Scraptoft Lane, LEICESTER
Tel: 0116 2769401

Nuffield Hospital-Nottingham
748 Mansfield Road, Woodthorpe, NOTTINGHAM
Tel: 0115 9209209

The Lincoln Nuffield Hospital
LINCOLN
Tel: 01522 578000

Hynotherapy

Ambrose Bryning
LEICESTER
Tel: 0116 2552689

Armstrong Prior
LEICESTER
Tel: 0116 2764911

Fiona Biddell
16 St. Phillip Road, Burton on the Wolds,
Wymeswold, LEICESTER
Tel: 01509 881411
*Hypno Birthing for easier, safer and more
comfortable birthday.*

G Wellington-Spur
LEICESTER
Tel: 0116 2671519

Helen C. Ottaway-Foster
WARKS
Tel: 024 76490149

Hypnotherapy Works
LEICESTER
Tel: 0116 2602312
Web: www.hypnotherapy-works.com

Jane Snookes
LEICESTER
Tel: 0116 2991978

Jaqui Crooks
LEICESTER
Tel: 0116 2865983
Email: jaqui@beaconhypno.fsnet.co.uk
Web: www.beaconhypno.fsnet.co.uk

Mind & Body
LEICESTER
Tel: 0871 2300039
Web: ww.mind-body.co.uk

Mind Body and Harmony Ltd
LEICESTER
Tel: 01455 553054
Email: info@mindbbodyharmony.ltd.uk
Web: www.mindbbodyharmony.ltd.uk

National Council for Hypnotherapy
LEICESTER
Tel: 01509 881477

Samantha Walsh
LEICESTER
Tel: 0116 2990136

Sterry-Blunt Mark
LEICESTER
Tel: 01572 812555

Susan Parker
NORTHAMPTON
Tel: 01858 575675

The Eastgate Health Centre
LEICESTER
Tel: 0116 2511647

Turning Pebbles
132 Wollaton Road, Beeston, NOTTINGHAM
Tel: 0115 9135104
Web: www.turningstones.co.uk

Internet Directories

www.babiesbaskets.com
www.monsterparties.co.uk
www.bearing-gifts.com
www.chatsonline.co.uk
www.colybernardi.co.uk
www.eatergreens.com
www.funkyegg.com
www.hippychick.com
www.juniorpetunia.com
www.justjellycat.co.uk
www.kidscavern.com
www.limiteds.com
www.littletrekkers.co.uk
www.malthouse-hunter.com
www.minormail.co.uk
www.mynametags.com
www.newbabybaskets.co.uk
www.olimia.co.uk
www.partiespieces.co.uk
www.partydirectory4kids.co.uk
www.princesandprincesses.co.uk
www.puffandpumpkin.com
www.raindrops.co.uk
www.samandsid.co.uk
www.snuglo.com
www.thebabycloset.co.uk
www.thekatspyjamas.com
www.travellingwithchildren.co.uk
www.treasurehunt4kids.co.uk
www.whoopsadaisyltd.com

Able Hands Cleaning Services
DERBY
Tel: 01283 213505

Always Ironing
LEICESTER
Tel: 0116 2719662

Best Pressed Ironing Service
DERBY
Tel: 07977 691628

Brightwaters Launderette
NOTTINGHAM
Tel: 0115 9483097

Carlton Launderette
NOTTINGHAM
Tel: 0115 9878696

Chellaston Launderette
DERBY
Tel: 01332 703547

Countrywide Laundry Services Ltd
LEICS
Tel: 01530 458898

Dolly Tub Ironing Services
DERBYS
Tel: 01773 824200

Executive Ironing Services
DERBY
Tel: 01332 731476

Express Ironing
DERBYS
Tel: 0115 9307436

Full Steam Ahead
NOTTINGHAM
Tel: 0115 8548473

Iron Maidens
NOTTINGHAM
Tel: 0115 9459032

Ironing Systems Ltd
NOTTINGHAM
Tel: 0115 9605485

Its Brilliant
NOTTINGHAM
Tel: 0115 9140013

Kerry's Professional Ironing Service
DERBYS
Tel: 01335 343914

Liz's Laundry
NOTTINGHAM
Tel: 0115 9280833

Needs Pressing
DERBYS
Tel: 07970 460826

Oakwood Ironing Services
DERBY
Tel: 01332 664126

Press Gang
NOTTINGHAM
Tel: 0115 9397987

Press On
DERBY
Tel: 01283 568390

Pressed Express
NOTTINGHAM
Tel: 0115 9602185

Pressing Matters
DERBYS
Tel: 01332 870157

**Prestige Cleaning
& Ironing Services**
STAFFS
Tel: 01283 525905

Spare Hands
DERBY
Tel: 01332 872188

The Iron Inn
NOTTINGHAM
Tel: 0115 9191089

The Ironing Bored
LEICS
Tel: 0116 2812748

The Ironing Lady
DERBY
Tel: 01773 880116

The Ironing Service
LEICS
Tel: 01530 836437

The Steamshop
NOTTINGHAM
Tel: 0115 9212580

HALLAM
FINE JEWELLERY

THE CIRCLE OF LIFE

Like the wedding ring, the eternity ring is a symbol of love that lasts forever; a simple circle of metal with no beginning and no end. It's the perfect gift to celebrate the birth of your first baby and your enduring commitment to each other.

As a concept, the eternity ring goes back centuries with the earliest known example found in Ur (in modern-day Iraq) dating from 4000BC. The tradition then continued through history with the plain bands favoured by the Egyptians and ancient Greeks. But many people nowadays take inspiration from Celtic multi-stranded or plaited designs, or the Elizabethan idea of a snake swallowing its tail.

Because it's an evolution of a wedding ring, an eternity ring is also usually worn on your ring finger (although you can really wear it on any finger you like!) but there's no hard and fast rule as to which order you should wear your rings in. Many women never remove their wedding rings so that's the first ring they put on. Whether you then wear your eternity ring second and engagement ring third, or vice versa, is usually down to the design of the ring – whichever place it fits most comfortably – and your personal preference.

There are lots of opinions about when's the right time to give and receive an eternity ring and really it's up to the individual couple to decide (although from a female point of view, don't make us wait an eternity!) Some people favour the first wedding anniversary (it's a lot better than paper!) but in fact, as the ring symbolises the husband's continuing love for his wife, it's the perfect gift for any anniversary. It's also a beautiful way of celebrating the birth of a first child and re-emphasising a couple's commitment to each other at this happy time.

According to Stuart Thexton, MD of Hallam Fine Jewellery, "Eternity rings have become extremely popular with our customers in the last few years. A lot of husbands and couples come to us looking for a way to commemorate the birth of their first child and celebrate their love, and a stone-studded eternity ring is the perfect solution."

Unless you opt for a style of ring that's based on a historical design, most modern eternity rings take the form of a plain band set with a row of gemstones of the same size and cut. A 'full' eternity ring is when the stones are set all the way around the shank. This means that the size of the ring can't be adjusted so it needs to be custom-made for you. A 'half' eternity ring is when the stones are set only on the front half of the ring, sometimes with a raised stone in the centre. Many women find half rings more comfortable to wear and that's because the band between the fingers doesn't have to be as thick as with a full ring as it doesn't need to accommodate any stones.

Stuart Thexton of Hallam Fine Jewellery adds: "There really aren't any set rules about the design of an eternity ring – you can have exactly what you want! Traditionally, diamonds have been the most popular choice but these days couples are getting more creative. Pink sapphires for a baby girl and blue sapphires for a boy are a lovely choice. Birth and astrological stones are also becoming more popular.

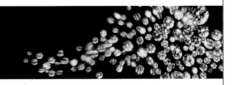

You don't have to stick to just one band of stones - two or three bands of different coloured stones look very stylish. And you don't have to be restricted to round, brilliant-cut stones. Emerald or princess cut stones are particularly good for eternity rings because they can be set edge-to-edge in a continuous line."

So basically, anything goes! Gold, platinum or silver bands and a huge choice of precious and semi-precious stones make it easy to design a ring that symbolises your own particular relationship. But it also makes it harder to narrow down your choice. That's why many couples like to choose a combination of birth stones to reflect the very special relationship between both partners and their new baby.

Birth stones became fashionable in the eighteenth century and you may have noticed that there are lots of variations on which stone goes with which month. But here's the definitive version, as agreed by the National Association of Goldsmiths in 1937.

Month	Stone	Colour
January	Garnet	Deep red
February	Amethyst	Deep purple
March	Aquamarine	Pale blue
April	Diamond	Clear
May	Emerald	Intense green
June	Pearl	Pale cream
July	Ruby	Red
August	Peridot	Shades of green
September	Sapphire	Blue, pink or yellow
October	Opal	Various
November	Topaz	Yellow
December	Turquoise	Pale blue

If your eternity ring is going to be a plain band featuring stones set around the shank then you'll probably find that pearl and opal aren't suitable because they're too soft.

Whatever stone or combination of stones and settings you choose, an eternity ring should be something completely unique and personal to you and your partner. A meaningful, permanent reminder of your love and commitment to each other that will last forever.

Come to Hallam

Hallam Fine Jewellery is a leading retailer in the East Midlands representing the world's finest jewellers and luxury watchmakers. As well as elegance, exclusivity, inspiration and style, Hallam's customers are provided with the highest quality products and customer service available. Whatever your taste: from timeless traditional through to chic contemporary, be inspired.

For further information telephone Hallam on 0115 941 1276

or visit www.hallamfinejewellery.com

Bringing Children out of their shells

Mercury House, Shipstone Business Centre,
Northgate, New Basford NG7 7SN
Tel: 0115 9648222

Mariquitas
NOTTINGHAM
Tel: 0115 9604323

El Club Espanol
Mercury House,
Shipstone Business Centre
NOTTINGHAM
Tel: 0115 964 8222

La Jolie Ronde
43 Long Acre, Bingham,
NOTTS
Tel: 01949 839715

Le Club Francais
Mercury House,
Shipstone Business Centre
NOTTINGHAM
Tel: 0115 964 8222

The Language Tutor
LEICESTER
Tel: 0116 270 5919
Spanish, French, Portuguese and Italian.

Left-Handedness

www.anythingleft-handed.co.uk

www.left-handersday.com

With over 3,000 centres in the UK, Le Club Francais
leads in languages through school clubs, business
tuition and supplying teachers and resources to schools.

Contact: Sara Bishop
Tel Number(s): 01158 465 834
Email: frenchnottingham@leclubfrancais.com

Albion Leisure Centre
DERBYS
Tel: 0115 9440200

Ashbourne Leisure Centre
Ashbourne, DERBYS
Tel: 01332 343712

Aylestone Leisure Centre
LEICESTER
Tel: 0116 2333040

Belper Leisure Centre
Belper, DERBYS
Tel: 01773 825285

Bramcote Leisure Centre
Derby Road, Bramcote,
NOTTINGHAM
Tel: 0115 917 3000
Web: www.broxtowe.gov.uk

Braunstone Recreation Centre
LEICESTER
Tel: 0116 2333085

Broxtowe Borough Council
NOTTINGHAM
Tel: 0115 9177777

Calverton Leisure Centre
Flatts Lane, Calverton,
NOTTINGHAM
Tel: 0115 9653781
Email: calverton@gedling.gov.uk
Web: www.gedling.gov.uk
Fun packed children's holiday activities available all day Monday - Friday for 5-16 year olds. For further information contact the centre.

Carlton Forum
NOTTINGHAM
Tel: 0115 9872333

Charnwood Leisure Centre
LEICESTER
Tel: 01509 611080

Chester Green Community Group
DERBY
Tel: 01332 360342

Chilwell Olympia Sports Centre
NOTTINGHAM
Tel: 0115 9173333

Clifton Leisure Centre
NOTTINGHAM
Tel: 0115 9152333

Coalville Gymnastics
COALVILLE
Tel: 01530 811001

Cossington Street Sports Centre
LEICESTER
Tel: 0116 2333060

Cotgrave Leisure Centre
Woodview, Cotgrave NOTTINGHAM
Tel: 0115 9892916

Earl Shilton Social Institute
LEICESTER
Tel: 01455 847273

East Leake Leisure Centre
LEICESTER
Tel: 01509 852956

Eastwood Community Sports Centre
NOTTINGHAM
Tel: 01773 770099

Elizabeth Park Sports & Community Centre
LEICESTER
Tel: 0116 2602519

Enderby Leisure Centre
LEICESTER
Tel: 0116 2750234

Etwall Leisure Centre
Etwall, DERBYS
Tel: 01283 733348

Evington Swimming Pool
LEICESTER
Tel: 0116 2995575

**Fleckney Sports
& Leisure Centre**
LEICESTER
Tel: 0116 2403755

Goals Soccer Centre Ltd
LEICESTER
Tel: 0116 2490555

**Greasley Community
& Sports Centre**
NOTTS
Tel: 01773 760072

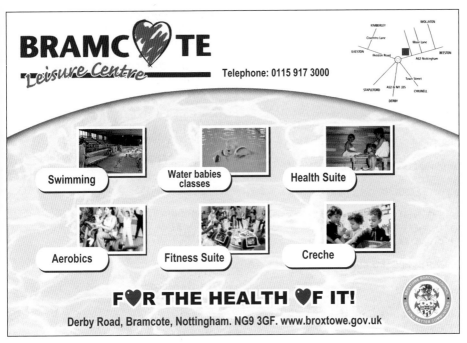

BRAMC♥TE Leisure Centre

Telephone: 0115 917 3000

Swimming

Water babies classes

Health Suite

Aerobics

Fitness Suite

Creche

F♥R THE HEALTH ♥F IT!

Derby Road, Bramcote, Nottingham. NG9 3GF. www.broxtowe.gov.uk

**Green Bank
Leisure Centre**
Swadlincote, DERBYS
Tel: 01332 297444

**Greens Health
& Fitness**
LEICESTER
Tel: 0116 2612333

**Harborough
Leisure Centre**
LEICESTER
Tel: 01858 410115

**Harvey Hadden
Sports Centre**
NOTTINGHAM
Tel: 0115 9151515

Heanor Leisure Centre
DERBYS
Tel: 01773 769711

Hermitage Leisure Centre
LEICESTER
Tel: 01530 811215

Hood Park Leisure Centre
LEICESTER
Tel: 0116 4122181

Hucknall Leisure Centre
NOTTS
Tel: 0115 9568750

Huncote Leisure Centre
LEICESTER
Tel: 0116 2750246

John Carroll Leisure Centre
NOTTINGHAM
Tel: 0115 9151535

Keyworth Leisure centre
NOTTINGHAM
Tel: 0115 9375582

Kibworth Sports Centre
LEICESTER
Tel: 0116 2796971

Kimberley Leisure Centre
NOTTINGHAM
Tel: 0115 9173366

Leicester Leys Leisure Centre
LEICESTER
Tel: 0116 2333070

Lenton Leisure Centre
NOTTINGHAM
Tel: 0115 9150095

Meadowside Leisure Centre
Burton-On-Trent
Tel: 01283 508865

Megazone Laser Centre
LEICESTER
Tel: 0116 2531153

Melbourne Leisure Centre
Melbourne, DERBYS
Tel: 01332 863522

Melton Leisure Centre
LEICESTER
Tel: 01664 851111

Mowmacre Community & Sports Centre
LEICESTER
Tel: 0116 2352480

New Park Leisure Centre
LEICESTER
Tel: 0116 2333080

Noel Street Leisure Centre
NOTTS
Tel: 0115 9151545

Nottingham Tennis Centre
NOTTINGHAM
Tel: 0115 9150000

Notts Tots
NOTTINGHAM
Tel: 0115 915 2726
Web: www.nottingham.gov.uk/leisurecentres

Parklands
LEICESTER
Tel: 0116 2720789

Portland Leisure Centre
NOTTINGHAM
Tel: 0115 9150015

Powerleague
NOTTINGHAM
Tel: 0115 9867890

Queens Leisure Centre
Derby
Tel: 01332 716620

Redhill Leisure Centre
NOTTINGHAM
Tel: 0115 9569996

Richard Herrod Leisure Centre
NOTTINGHAM
Tel: 0115 9612949

Rushcliffe Arena
Rugby Road, West Bridgford, NOTTINGHAM
Tel: 0115 9814027
*Childrens indoor soft play area and after school
club, great venue for children's parties.*

Rushcliffe Leisure Centre
Boundary Road, West Bridgford, NOTTINGHAM
Tel: 0115 9234921
Web: www.rushcliffe.gov.uk

Sandiacre Freisland Sports Centre
NOTTINGHAM
Tel: 0115 9490400

Sarvodya Samaj
LEICESTER
Tel: 0116 2540387

Selston Leisure Centre
NOTTS
Tel: 01773 781800

Shobnall Leisure Centre
Burton-On-Trent
Tel: 01283 516180

Southfields Drive Sports Centre
LEICESTER
Tel: 0116 2839047

Southglade Leisure Centre
NOTTS
Tel: 0115 9151595

Southwell Leisure Centre
NOTTINGHAM
Tel: 01636 813000

Spence Street Sport Centre
LEICESTER
Tel: 0116 2995584

Sport In Desford Clubhouse
LEICESTER
Tel: 01455 828786

Sports-League Leicester Ltd
LEICESTER
Tel: 0116 2470221

Springwood Leisure Centre
Derby
Tel: 01332 664433

Squash Leicester
LEICESTER
Tel: 0116 2703811

St. Margarets Pastures
LEICESTER
Tel: 0116 2333095

The Bingham Leisure Centre
NOTTS
Tel: 01949 838628

The Cornerhouse
NOTTINGHAM
Tel: 0115 9505168

Victoria Leisure Centre
NOTTINGHAM
Tel: 0115 9155600

Victoria Park Leisure Centre
DERBYS
Tel: 0115 9440400

West Park Leisure Centre
NOTTINGHAM
Tel: 0115 9461400

Wigston Swimming Pool
LEICESTER
Tel: 0116 2881758

Willows Sports Centre
Derby
Tel: 01332 204004

Bon Nuit Ltd
NOTTINGHAM
Tel: 01636 642834
Web: www.bon-nuit.com

Cot Beds Direct
6 Park Lane, Castle Donington, DERBYS
Tel: 01332 812825
Only official reseller of Tutti Bambini nursery furniture in the East Midlands.

Nik Nak Toys
The Lodge, Eastend, Damerham, HAMPSHIRE
Tel: 0845 644 7025
Web: www.niknaktoys.co.uk
Imaginative fun and affordable wood and soft toys for children. Buy on line, mail order or catalogue.

Vertbaudet
BRADFORD
Tel: 0500 012345
Web: www.vertbaudet.co.uk

Massage
See Baby Massage

Jodie House Massage Therapist
NOTTINGHAM
Tel: 0115 9625888

Maternity Websites

www.apeainthepod.com
www.bloomingmarvellous.co.uk
www.broodyhens.co.uk
www.budget-bumps.com
www.jojomamanbebe.co.uk
www.mamasandpapas.co.uk
www.motherhood.com
www.vertbaudet.co.uk

Maternity Wear

Blooming Marvellous
PO BOX 730A,
SURBITON
Tel: 0870 751 8977
Web: www.bloomingmarvellous.co.uk
The widest range of exclusive maternity fashion in the UK plus gorgeous babywear and the best nursery essentials and baby toys. For a free catalogue call the number below or shop online or find your nearest store at www.bloomingmarvellous.co.uk

Formes (UK) Ltd
12 Exchange Arcade,
NOTTINGHAM
Tel: 0115 9585550
Contemporary fashion for the pregnant woman.

Jo Jo Maman Bebe
Distribution House, Oxwich Road,
Newport, SOUTH WALES
Tel: 0870 241 0560
Web: www.jojomamanbebe.co.uk
*Extremely Stylish maternity wear at reasonable
prices, plusl underwear, nursery goods and
children's clothing.*

Proud 2b Maternity Boutique
5 Loseby Lane, LEICESTER
Tel: 0116 2621127
Maternity wear and accessories.

Push Maternity Wear
9 Therberton Street, LONDON
Tel: 020 7359 2003
Email: enquiries@pushmaternity.com
Web: pushmaternity.com

Swells Maternity Wear
Newark Road, Alverton, NOTTS
Tel: 01949 850263
Web: www.swells.co.uk

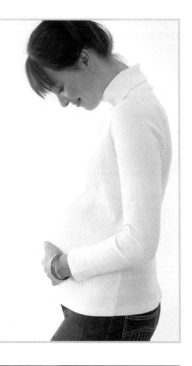

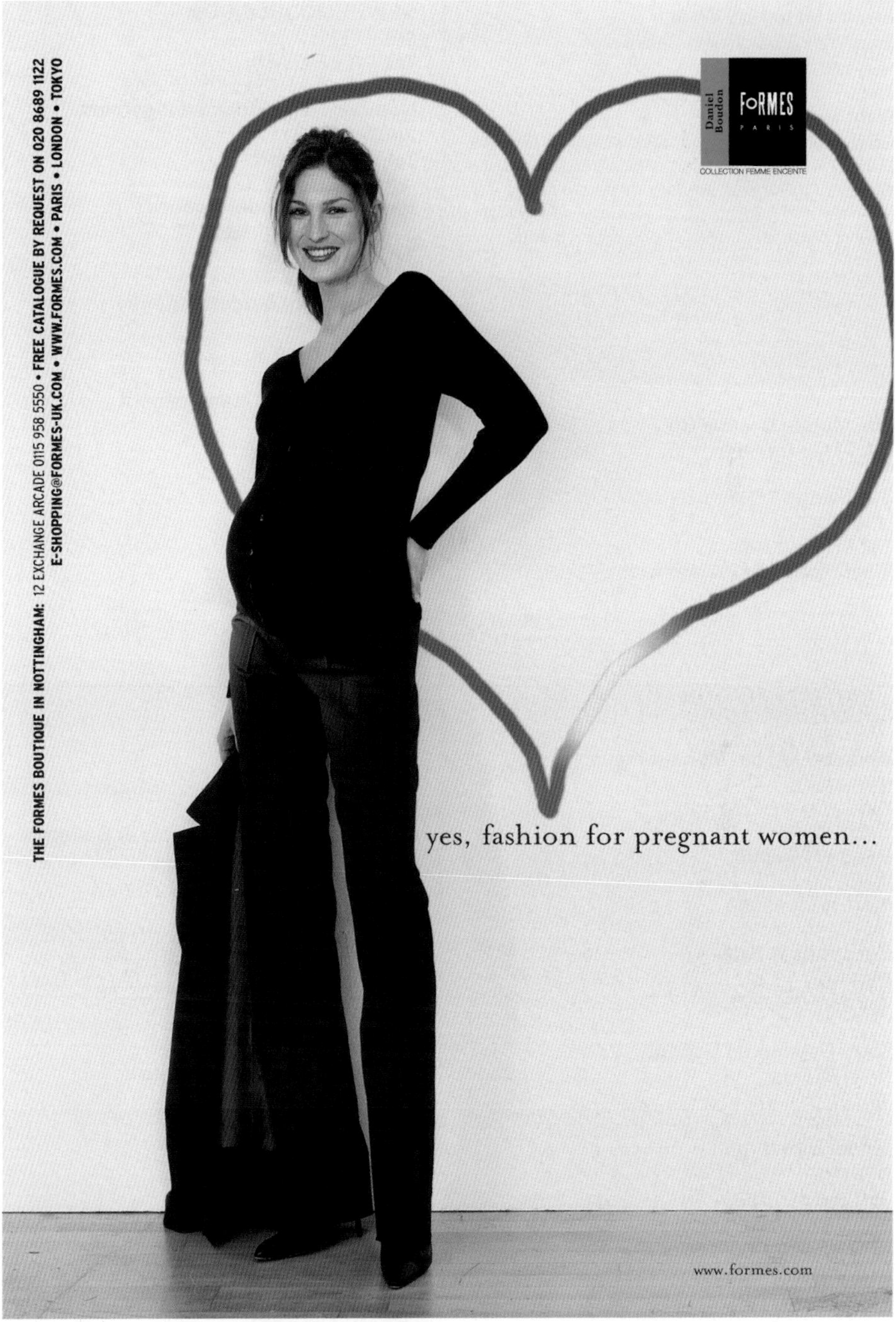

THE FORMES BOUTIQUE IN NOTTINGHAM: 12 EXCHANGE ARCADE 0115 958 5550 • FREE CATALOGUE BY REQUEST ON 020 8689 1122
E-SHOPPING@FORMES-UK.COM • WWW.FORMES.COM • PARIS • LONDON • TOKYO
Daniel Boudon
FORMES
PARIS
COLLECTION FEMME ENCEINTE
yes, fashion for pregnant women...
www.formes.com

Swells Maternity Wear
Drury Walk, Broadmarsh Centre
NOTTINGHAM
Tel: 0115 9470408
Web: www.swells.co.uk
Established 16 years ago, Swells offers 6 different European fashion collections for all tastes and occasions. Our staff are fully trained to fit the 4 pre-natal and nursing bra ranges and offer a high level of personal service advice when needed.

Mobile Creche

The Mobile Creche Co.
Tel: 01423 797440

Scalliwags
LEICESTER
Tel: 0116 2813469
Email: scalliwags2002@aol.com

Model Agencies

Absolute Model Management
LIVERPOOL
Tel: 08702 403375

Destiny Models
LEICS
Tel: 01530 263877

Euro Kids & Kids
DERBYS
Tel: 0871 750 1575

Mary Gay Model School
NOTTINGHAM
Tel: 0115 9607664

Model Direct
DERBYS
Tel: 08705 010101

Models Direct
NOTTINGHAM
Tel: 08705 010101

NEWUKMODELS.COM
SHEFFIELD
Tel: 0114 2500867

Number One Model Management
BIRMINGHAM
Tel: 0115 9240055

Pat Keeling Model Agency
LEICESTER
Tel: 01162 622540

Rising Talent Models Agency
NOTTINGHAM
Tel: 0870 8300679

Stanleys Model Management
DERBYS
Tel: 01332 875880

Tuesday Child
MACCLESFIELD
Tel: 01625 612244

Uk Models Nottingham
NOTTINGHAM
Tel: 0115 9105610

Museums
See also Tourist Attractions

Nottingham City Museums & Galleries
NOTTINGHAM
Tel: 0115 9152731

Music Schools & Teachers

A Wilmott Guitar and Flute
Derby
Tel: 01332 776931

Barrie Nisbet
Eastwood
Tel: 01773 762173

Brenda Hall
NOTTINGHAM
Tel: 0115 9332498

C Bell
NOTTINGHAM
Tel: 0115 9812547

C Buxton
NOTTS
Tel: 01773 762173

Caterpillar Music
11 Tomson Avenue, Ratcliffe-On-Trent,
NOTTINGHAM
Tel: 0115 8416949

Charnwood Music Guitar Tuition
LOUGHBOROUGH
Tel: 01509 237327

Chloe Willson
LEICESTER
Tel: 0116 2101311

D.R. Drum Tuition
LEICESTER
Tel: 0116 2592950

Dance Doctors Studio
NOTTINGHAM
Tel: 0115 946 4822

David Rose Piano Tuition
LEICESTER
Tel: 0116 2571909

Derby Music Association
DERBY
Tel: 01332 558007

EPTA
Swadlincote
Tel: 01283 224445
East Midland Tuition
NOTTS
Tel: 07901 685051

Expert Tuition
DERBYS
Tel: 01332 200149

Elizabeth Paling
LOUGHBOROUGH
Tel: 07711 399856

Farndale Music
NOTTS
Tel: 01623 552023

Fox's Yamaha Music School
NOTTINGHAM
Tel: 0115 9411556

Frederick Parnell School Of Music
NOTTINGHAM
Tel: 0115 9473251

Gary Fraser Lewis BA Hons
NOTTINGHAM
Tel: 0115 9606605

Glen Hughes Piano Tuition
LEICESTER
Tel: 0116 2249290

H Frost
NOTTINGHAM
Tel: 0115 9233644

Hazel Caswell LRAM
NOTTINGHAM
Tel: 0115 9233849

Ian Crabtree
LEICESTER
Tel: 0116 2543857

Ian MacDonald
NOTTINGHAM
Tel: 0115 8776106

Jay I
LEICESTER
Tel: 01530 262528

Jo Jingles Pre-School
Music & Movement
Coalville
Tel: 01530 814083

Maria Bohdan Piano Tuition
NOTTINGHAM
Tel: 07931 704408

Martin Cobley
NOTTINGHAM
Tel: 0115 9259837

Michael Bonshor
Melton Mowbray
Tel: 01664 850681

Mickleover School of Music
DERBY
Tel: 01332 519402

Mike Rushton
Glenfield
Tel: 0116 2870315

Miss Rosemary Wright
Leicester
Tel: 0116 2777631

Modern Singing
NOTTINGHAM
Tel: 0115 8400760

Mrs P Young
NOTTINGHAM
Tel: 0115 9692179

Music with Mummy
STAFFS
Tel: 01889 568880

Musical Mini's
38 Pierrepont Road, West Bridgford,
NOTTINGHAM
Tel: 0115 8469297
Email: liz@musicalminis.co.uk
Web: www.musicalminis.co.uk
*The fun time music group for babies and toddlers
from 6 months to pre-school.*

Musical Youth
Leicester
Tel: 0116 2835615

Nottingham Woodwind Studio
NOTTS
Tel: 0115 9264425

Opus
DERBY
Tel: 01332 294750

Orchard School of Music
NOTTTINGHAM
Tel: 0115 9670811

P Skinner
Burton-On-Trent
Tel: 01283 702143

Paul Hollis
NOTTINGHAM
Tel: 0115 9725678

Piano and Keyboard Tuition
Leicester
Tel: 0116 2127986

Richard Eaton
NOTTINGHAM
Tel: 0115 9336494

Richard Woodward
NOTTINGHAM
Tel: 0115 9609421

Robert Doughty
NOTTINGHAM
Tel: 0115 9670391

Roger Carrington
NOTTINGHAM
Tel: 0115 9293151

Rowland Nelken
NOTTINGHAM
Tel: 0115 8400354

Ruby Ellensen
Market Harborough
Tel: 01858 525352

Sarah Simmonds
NOTTINGHAM
Tel: 0115 9423337

Sherwood Music School
NOTTINGHAM
Tel: 0115 9621144

Sillitoe Drum Studio
NOTTINGHAM
Tel: 0115 9870707

Stella Middleton
NOTTINGHAM
Tel: 0115 9233133

Susan Lake
NOTTINGHAM
Tel: 0115 9133627

The Belvoir Piano Academy
NOTTINGHAM
Tel: 07971 846990

The Voice Box
Derby
Tel: 01332 295297

Tim Brown Orum
Loughborough
Tel: 01509 413891

Underground Music Studios
NOTTINGHAM
Tel: 07966 462138

Wardle Singing Tuition
Coalville
Tel: 01530 839828

Waynes Guitar Shack
NOTTINGHAM
Tel: 0115 9616452

Yamaha Music School
DERBY
Tel: 01332 206706

Zawawi Music
Leicester
Tel: 07771 968176

Zoe Brecht
NOTTINGHAM
Tel: 0115 9233017

Easy2name
Tel: 01635 298326
Email: www.easy2name.com

Stuck On You
Tel: 0845 456 0014
Web: www.stuckonyou.biz

Nanny Services

1st Leicestershire Nanny Agency
LEICESTER
Tel: 0116 2661800
Web: www.leicestershirenannies.co.uk

1st Premier Au-Pair Agency
NR STOURPORT
Tel: 01299 828383
Web: www.premieraupair.co.uk

Abacus Au Pair Agency
BRIGHTON
Tel: 01273 203803
Email: info@abacusaupairagency.co.uk
Web: www.abacusaupairagency.co.uk

**Antionettes Aupair &
Nanny Agency UK**
TRURO
Tel: 0800 1696568
Email: antionettes@btopenworld.com
Web: www.childcare-agancy.co.uk

ATA Au Pairs.co.uk
BRIGG
Tel: 01652 655969
Web: www.ataaupairs.co.uk

Au Pair Express
NOTTINGHAM
Tel: 0115 8415604

Au Pairs 4 You
NOTTINGHAM
Tel: 0845 065 6665

Beasley Childminders
LEICESTER
Tel: 01455 444176

Brick Au Pair Recruitment
SHEFFIELD
Tel: 0114 2760564

Care-On-Line
NOTTINGHAM
Tel: 01949 843332
Email: nannies.aupairs@care-on-line.com
Web: www.care-on-line.com

Childminding Information
LEICESTER
Tel: 0116 2656545

Dawn Page
LEICESTER
Tel: 01509 551235

East Midlands Au Pair Agency Ltd
NOTTINGHAM
Tel: 0115 8460044

**Emma Hudson - Beaver
Reg Childminder**
LEICESTER
Tel: 0116 2888510

Fox G
LEICESTER
Tel: 0116 2243914

Imperial Nannies
LONDON
Tel: 0207 795 6220

Janette Bott
LEICESTER
Tel: 01509 816745

L Muirhead
LEICESTER
Tel: 0116 2336846

Nanny Search
Tel: 0208 348 4111
Web: www.nanny-search.co.uk

nannytax
BRIGHTON
Tel: 0845 226 2203

Northern Au Pair Agency
MANCHESTER
Tel: 0161 740 1828
Email: napa@onetel.net.uk
Web: www.onetel.net.uk

Nottinghamshire Nannies
Gibsmere House, Gibsmere, NOTTINGHAM
Tel: 01636 830898
Web: www.notttsnannies.co.uk
Hours of business Monday-Friday
10.00 am-3.00 pm. Mobile: 07929 982618

Pearson Stacey
LEICESTER
Tel: 01509 213545

Thompson's Childminding
LEICESTER
Tel: 01455 449954

Nappies

Bushra Finch
266 Wyggeston Street, Burton On Trent,
DERBY
Tel: 01283 535818
Web: www.firstbreathdoulas.co.uk
Cotton nappies, nursing bras, slings, homeopathic
remedy kits and more!

Local Cloth Nappy Consultant
4 Primrose Avenue, Newark NOTTS
Tel: 01636 687925

Nappy Hopper Laundry
Laundering Service
Unit 1a, Nash Lane North, Hykeham, LINCOLN
Tel: 01522 684495
Web: WWW.NAPPYHOPPER.CO.UK

Nature Babies Real Nappies Limited
Unit 17, Clear View Farm, Quorn, Loughborough
Tel: 01509 621879
Email: contact@naturebabies.co.uk
Web: www.naturebabies.co.uk
Creating a cleaner future for your baby, whether
washing at home, or using our laundry wash
service. Whatever your circumstances/budget we
will find a leak proof, hassle free system to suit you.

Nurseries

A1 Evington Nursery
LEICESTER
Tel: 0116 2738830

Abracadabra Pre-School Nursery
LEICESTER
Tel: 0116 2223377

Ace Childcare & Training Centre
DERBY
Tel: 01332 774255

Acorns Childrens Centre
The Old School Room, Church Street,
Lambley, NOTTINGHAM
Tel: 0115 9312745
Private Day Nursery. Registered from 6 weeks
onwards - includes BSC and ASC.

Adbolton Kindergarton
The Lodge, Adbolton Lane, NOTTINGHAM
Tel: 0115 9820101

Alfizz Childcare
Church Street, Alfreton, DERBY
Tel: 01773 522406
Email: sharon.brewer@btconnect.com
Friendly environment providing childcare for 2-14
year olds. Preschool care 2-5 year olds. Full day
care 3&4 year olds. Breakfast,after school and
holiday care for 3 14 year olds. For further details
please contact Alfizz.

Allexton Day Nursery
LEICESTER
Tel: 0116 2235582

Alphabet House Day Nursery
NOTTINGHAM
Tel: 0115 9734442

Alphabet Kids Nursery
84 Oakland Avenue, LEICESTER
Tel: 0116 2610393
Email: iluvkids@hotmail.com
Web: www.hotmail.com
A caring small sized nursery where children of all ages
play together, giving your children happy & enjoyable
memories. Children from 6 weeks to 8 years.

Nature Babies

Nature Babies is a small design, manufacture, wholesale and retail business originally started in 2001 by Isobel Parr who had used terry nappies and plastic pants on her first baby. When second baby arrived 10 years later, there were hardly any real nappy products around and certainly not without a trip down to a major shopping centre.

Starting by looking at various nappies on the market which had tobe tracked down by "Sherlock Holmes" type methods, one thing led to another and Nature Babies now occupies two units and employs 5 people, with sales growing every year. Nature Babies has a complete range of nappies to suit every situation and pocket, from terry nappies at £11.99 per dozen to gorgeous designer wraps or birth to potty fitted nappies and Stuffables - which are an innovative type of pocket nappy, which can be "stuffed" for as much or as little absorabcy as required, but removed again for easy laundering.

Nature Babies owner Isobel says "The washable nappy choices on the market can be confusing for a new mum, but we are always available for advice should washable nappies be a choice for you. It really is worth making the change, and we are here to help you to do so!" Isobel or her partner Jay can be contacted on **01509 621879** during weekdays and meanwhile here are some intersting nappy facts to turn you on to washable nappies.

Every £1 spent on single use nappies costs the Council Tax payer 10p to dispose of them. The total cost nationally for the disposal of nappies is £40 million each year.

The environment

8 million disposable nappies are thrown away in Britain every day. Over two and a half years, 6,000 disposable nappies will be used by one baby as opposed to re-using the same 24-50 "real" nappies.

Every £1 spent on single use nappies costs the Council Tax payer 10p to dispose of them. The total cost nationally for the disposal of nappies is £40 million each year. Disposables use 90 times more non-renewable material, for example, one cup of crude oil is needed to make one disposable nappy. To keep one baby in disposable nappies for two and a half years, four and a half trees will be cut down to produce the nappies.

Re-usable nappies are soft, cotton and breathable, which helps to prevent nappy rash. Disposable nappies contain gels and chemicals which are not subject to governmental controls or independent testing

Phone: 01509 621 065 or 621 879
email: contact@naturebabies.co.uk
web: www.naturebabies.co.uk.

We'll look after your little angels

ANGELS BY DAY

Hucknall Lane • Nottingham

- Before school, after school and holiday care available for 4-11 year olds
- Nursery care available for 0-5 year olds

For more info call

0115 9 519 915

Alton Manor Private Day Nursery
DERBY
Tel: 01773 829242

Angels by Day
Hillside House, Derby Road NOTTINGHAM
Tel: 0115 9789980

Angels by Day
NOTTS
Tel: 0115 9519915

Animal Crackers Childrens Nursery
DERBYS
Tel: 01283 791030

Apple Tree Day Nursery & Kids Club
LEICESTER
Tel: 01530 249872

Applecroft Nursery School
LEICESTER
Tel: 0116 2718277

Appleton Day Nursery
NOTTS
Tel: 01636 613833

Arboretum Nursery School
NOTTINGHAM
Tel: 0115 9151395

Ark Day Nursery
NOTTINGHAM
Tel: 0115 9624594
Web: www.childcarenottingham.co.uk

Arnold House Day Nursery
NOTTINGHAM
Tel: 0115 9666123

Ashby Castle Day Nursery
LEICESTER
Tel: 01530 415541

Ashby Day Nursery
LEICS
Tel: 01530 416622

Asquith Day Nursey
LEICESTER
Tel: 01455 234000

Asquith Nurseries
c/o David Lloyd Club, Aspley Lane,
NOTTINGHAM
Tel: 0115 9298035

Asquith Nurseries-Derby
David Lloyd Leisure Pride Parkway
Pride Park, DERBY
Tel: 01332 372127

Babes to Tots
ASHBY-DE-LA-ZOUCH
Tel: 01530 564446

Balderton Village Day Nursery
NOTTS
Tel: 01636 704708

Beacon Hill Day Nursery
NOTTINGHAM
Tel: 01636 704823

Beauchamp College Day Nursery
LEICESTER
Tel: 0116 2729124

Beech Tree Nursery
LEICESTER
Tel: 0116 2791010

Beehive Private Day Nursery
NOTTINGHAM
Tel: 0115 9587392

Bingham Day Nursery
55 Long Acre, Bingham NOTTINGHAM
Tel: 01949 839242

Birstall Rainbow Nursery
68-74 Wanlip Lane, Birstall, LEICESTER
Tel: 0116 2671331
Web: www.birstallrainbow.co.uk
Friendly private day nursery, quality
childcare provided from birth to 6 years.
Open 8 am- 6 pm Mon-Fri.

Bitteswell Montessori
LEICESTER
Tel: 01455 556050

Blackberry Bush Nursery
LEICESTER
Tel: 0116 2788744

Blossoms Day Nurseries
LEICESTER
Tel: 0116 2448600

Blueberry Bush Nursery
LEICESTER
Tel: 0116 2714888-2774088

Bosworth College Day Nursery
LEICESTER
Tel: 01455 823889

Bramcote Leisure Centre
Derby Road, Bramcote NOTTINGHAM
Tel: 0115 917 3000
Web: www.broxtowe.gov.uk

Bramcote Village Day Nursery
NOTTINGHAM
Tel: 0115 9430053
Web: www.bramcotevillagenursery.co.uk

Breaston Manor Day Nursery
DERBYS
Tel: 01332 874544

Breedon House Childrens Centre
NOTTINGHAM
Tel: 0115 9732600

Bright Futures 2 Day Nursery
NOTTINGHAM
Tel: 0115 9121633

Bright Sparks Day Nursery
LEICESTER
Tel: 01455 234266

Brooksby Melton College Day Nursery
LEICESTER
Tel: 01664 480301

Brunts Farmhouse Day Nursery
LEICESTER
Tel: 01664 822188

Burton Day Nursery
DERBYS
Tel: 01283 568836

Bush Babies Childrens Nurseries Ltd
LEICESTER
Tel: 0116 2884046

Cared 4 Nottingham
19 Brookhill Street, Stapleford NOTTINGHAM
Tel: 0115 8492304
Email: info@cared4.co.uk
Web: www.cared4.co.uk
Private day nursery. Baby unit, pre-school and after school club.

Carey Days Day Nursery
NOTTINGHAM
Tel: 0115 9506530

Carlton & Gedling Day Nursery
NOTTINGHAM
Tel: 0115 9617083

Carrington Private Day Nursery
NOTTINGHAM
Tel: 0115 9691170

Castle Lane Day Nursery
LEICESTER
Tel: 01858 468006

Castle Meadow Nursery
NOTTINGHAM
Tel: 0115 9740008

Charnwood Day Nursery
LEICESTER
Tel: 01509 508012

Charnwood Nursery & Pre-School
22 Lonsdale Road, Thurmaston,
LEICESTER
Tel: 0116 2696162
Quality childcare for babies, toddlers, pre-school, grant funded children and out of school club (ages 4-11).

Cheeky Monkeys
STAFFS
Tel: 01889 564444

Cherry Tree Day Nursery
ETWALL
Tel: 01283 732297

Cherry Tree Nursery & Kids Club
LEICESTER
Tel: 01530 249872

Cherubs Day Nursery
Executive House, St Albans Road,
Bulwell, NOTTINGHAM
Tel: 0115 9795975
Email: cherubsnurseries@aol.com

Cherubs Day Nursery
Valeview, 362 St. Albans,
Bulwell, NOTTINGHAM
Tel: 0115 9795994

Cherubs Day Nursey
The High Street, Kimberley,
NOTTINGHAM
Tel: 0115 9389090

Cherubs Days Nursery
Grasmere North Road, North Muskham,
Newark, NOTTS
Tel: 01636 706525

Childcare East Midlands
AWARD WINNING NURSERIES
ACROSS NOTTINGHAMSHIRE

LONGDALE NURSERY SCHOOL & CHILDREN'S CENTRE 01623 491919

CHERUBS KIMBERLEY 01159 389090

CHERUBS NEWARK 01636 706525

CHERUBS EXECUTIVE HOUSE BULWELL 01159 795975

CHERUBS VALE VIEW BULWELL 01159 795994

CHERUBS CHILDCARE CENTRE MANSFIELD 01623 420940

- For Children of 6wks-5yrs Out of School clubs 3-11yrs
- **Established in 1993**
- Highest standards of care and education in a safe, secure and stimulating environment.
- Our staff are qualified and experienced. They are chosen for their caring friendly and professional manner, and vigorous checks are carried out on all our staff.
- Qualified cooks provide delicious nutritionally balanced meals.
- Separate units for each individual age group offering an excellent age specific range of toys and equipment
- Separate out of school clubs for 3 to 11 years
- **OPEN 51 WEEKS PER YEAR** 7.30am-6.00pm

Cherubs Childcare Centre
Welbeck Rd, mansfield Woodhouse
Tel: 01623 420940

Cherubs Day Nursery
Valeview, 362 St. Albans,
Bulwell, NOTTINGHAM
Tel: 0115 9795994

Cherubs Day Nursey
The High Street, Kimberley, NOTTINGHAM
Tel: 0115 9389090

Cherubs Days Nursery
Grasmere North Road, North Muskham,
Newark, NOTTS
Tel: 01636 706525

Children First at Breedon House
NOTTINGHAM
Tel: 0115 9733613

Childrens Corner
103 Loughborough Road, West Bridgford,
NOTTINGHAM
Tel: 0115 9815649
Web: www.childrens-corner.co.uk

Childs Play Day Nursery
NOTTINGHAM
Tel: 0115 9671542

Chuckle Bunnies
DERBY
Tel: 01283 539202

Church House Nursery
NOTTINGHAM
Tel: 0115 9677684

Cinders Day Nursery
NOTTINGHAM
Tel: 0115 9166331

City Nursery Ltd
LEICESTER
Tel: 0116 2470166

Clowns Nurseries
DERBYSHIRE
Tel: 01773 747983

**Clowns Private
Day Nursery**
NOTINGHAM
Tel: 0115 9390105

**Collingwood House
Day Nursery**
DERBY
Tel: 01283 537308

Est 1989

Children's corner

Fostering within children a sense of wonder and curiosity

6 weeks - 5yrs

103 Loughborough Road, West Bridgford,
Nottingham NG2 7JX • Tel: 0115 9815649
www.childrens-corner.co.uk • info@chidrens-corner.co.uk

Co-operative Day Nursery Ltd
NOTTINGHAM
Tel: 0115 9830003

Cottesmore Day Nursery
LEICESTER
Tel: 01572 812828

Croft Nursery School
NOTTINGHAM
Tel: 0115 9155812

Cromford Bridge Hall
DERBY
Tel: 01629 580238

Daisies Day Nursery
NOTTS
Tel: 0115 9665282

Daisy Chain Child Care
NOTTINGHAM
Tel: 0115 9791979

Daisy Chain Childrens Nursery
Eglantine, Rosa Park, Lutterworth Road,
BLABY, Leicester
Tel: 0116 2776506
Web: www.daisychainchildrensnursery.co.uk
Quality childcare set in rural area. Places individually tailored for children 0-8 years. A special place for your most precious possesion.

Daneshill Nursery
LEICESTER
Tel: 0116 2530856

De Verdun Childrens Day Nursery
LEICESTER
Tel: 01455 828853

Derby College
DERBY
Tel: 0800 028 0289

Derby Montessori School
DERBY
Tel: 01332 346333

Derwent Cottage Day Nursery
DERBY
Tel: 01332 663443

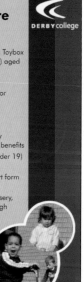

Derwent Stepping Stones Nursery
DERBYS
Tel: 01332 372245

Discovery Childcare
NOTTINGHAM
Tel: 0115 9384805

Discovery Day Nursery
DERBY
Tel: 01332 749052

Duncroft Nursery
NOTTINGHAM
Tel: 0115 9404491

Earl Shilton Montessori School
LEICESTER
Tel: 01455 841951

Early Learners Nursery School
LEICESTER
Tel: 0116 2511514

Early Start Nursery
The Nottinghamshire Royal Society for the Blind
Orzen Street, Radford, NOTTINGHAM
Tel: 0115 970 6806
Email: info@nrsb.org.uk
Web: www.nrsb.org.uk
An intergrated nursery for babies and children.

East Leake Day Nursery & Pre-School
Manor Farm Castle Hill, East Leake,
LEICESTER
Tel: 01509 854205

Edna G Olds Nursery
NOTTINGHAM
Tel: 0115 9156899

EduCare
NOTTINGHAM
Tel: 0115 9691700

Edwalton Nursery School
NOTTINGHAM
Tel: 0115 9452741

Fairy Tales Day Nursery
Manor Court, The Ford, Little Glen Road,
Glen Parva, LEICESTER
Tel: 0116 2788782
Web: www.fairytalesdaynursery.co.uk

Family First Ltd
The Croft Family Centre, Albert Road
Alexandra Park, NOTTINGHAM
Tel: 0115 9620772
Provides quality and affordable childcare. Toy and book library, sensory and soft play room.

First Class Day Nursery
Parkland Primary School Grounds
St. Thomas Road, South Wigston,
LEICESTER
Tel: 0116 2778829
Web: www.firstclassnursery.co.uk
Full time and part time places available all year round, including term time funded places for 3-4 year olds. We also charge hourly rates not sessional!

First Friends Private Day Nursery
141 Chaddesden Park Road,
Chaddesden, DERBYS
Tel: 01332 677660
Quality childcare from 3 months - 8 years - includes before & after school club and holiday club.

Established 1980

Loving • Stimulating • Educational

Adbolton Kindergarten
The Lodge, Adbolton Lane, West Bridgford, Nottingham NG2 5AS
Tel: 0115 982 0101

Bingham Day Nursery and Pre-School Centre
55 Long Acre, Bingham, Nottingham NG13 8AG
Tel: 01949 839242

East Leake Day Nursery, Pre-School, Out of School and Holiday Club
Manor Farm, Castle Hill, East Leake, Loughborough, LeicestershireLE 12 6LU
Tel: 01509 854205

Trent Fields Kindergarten, pre-School and Holiday Club
19/21 Trent Boulevard, West Bridgford, Nottingham NG2 5BB
Tel: 0115 982 1685

www.earlyyearschildcaregroup.co.uk
email: headoffice@earlyyearschildcaregroup.co.uk

Caring for your child's future

 City & Guilds
INVESTORS IN PEOPLE

Registered by OFSTED. Members of the National Day Nurseries Association

Fosse Paddock Kindergarton
Stragglethorpe, Radcliffe-On-Trent
NOTTINGHAM
Tel: 0115 9894226
Web: www.fossepaddock.com
Friendly Day Nursery set in idyllic countryside near Bingham and Radcliffe.

**Gateway Christian
School Nursery**
NOTTS
Tel: 0115 9303807

Gedling House Day Nursery
Wood Lane, Gedling, NOTTINGHAM
Tel: 0115 9552298
Web: www.GHDayNursery.com
Best of care in beautiful countryside surrounds.

Glebe Farm Nursery School
LEICESTER
Tel: 0116 2596883

Glebe Farm Nusery School
LEICESTER
Tel: 0116 2596883

Glebelands Pre-School & Out of School
LEICESTER
Tel: 0116 2362122

Goods Foundation Nursery
NOTTINGHAM
Tel: 0115 9872898

Gooseberry Bus Childrens Nursery
LEICESTER
Tel: 0116 2884046

Gooseberry Bush Day Nursery
NOTTINGHAM
Tel: 0115 9822220-9691696

Greenfields Community Day Nursery
NOTTINGHAM
Tel: 0115 8418441

Greenwood Day Nursery
NOTTINGHAM
Tel: 0115 9815061

Greenwood Infant School Nursery
NOTTINGHAM
Tel: 0115 9150183

Gwendolen Day Nursery
LEICESTER
Tel: 0116 2584966

Hanbury Kindergarten
LEICESTER
Tel: 01858 545788

Hand In Hand
NOTTINGHAM
Tel: 0115 9607217

Handkerchief Nursery
NOTTINGHAM
Tel: 01509 670394

Happy Hours
STAFFS
Tel: 01889 566678

Harlequins Private Day Nursery
1a George Street, Enderby LEICESTER
Tel: 0116 2750156

Harlequins Private Day Nursery
81 St Johns, Narborough, LEICESTER
Tel: 0116 2863045

Harrington Day Nursery
137 Belvedere Road, Burton On Trent, STAFFS
Tel: 01283 510882
Places available for children 6 weeks to 5 years in the nursery and up to 12 years for our adjoining after school club.

Heanor Day Nursery
DERBYS
Tel: 01773 531444

Henrys Day Nursery
NOTTINGHAM
Tel: 0115 9692282
Web: www.henrysdaynursery.co.uk

Hermitage Day Nursery
LEICS
Tel: 01530 814477

Hickory House Day Nursery
66-68 Loughborough Road,
West Bridgford, NOTTINGHAM
Tel: 0115 9142222

Highwood Day Nursery
54 Stanton Road, Stapenhill,
BURTON ON TRENT, Staffs
Tel: 01283 565069
Total day care for babies and children, before school care, after school care and holiday care.

Hillcrest Day Nursery
NOTTINGHAM
Tel: 0115 9604080

Hilltop Day Nursery
MEASHAM
Tel: 01530 274462

Hinckley Children & Family Centre
LEICESTER
Tel: 01455 637485

Hinckley Nursery
LEICESTER
Tel: 01455 234500

Hoar Cross Day Nursery
HOAR CROSS
Tel: 01283 575514

Hobby-Horse Nursery & Kids Club
NOTTS
Tel: 01636 525012

Hollies Day Nurseries
NOTTINGHAM
Tel: 0115 9606388

Holly Court Nursery School
Holly Court, Landmere Lane,
Edwalton, NOTTINGHAM
Tel: 0115 9845496
Quality childcare from 6 wks-5yrs.

Holmsdale Manor Nursery School
LEICESTER
Tel: 01530 262434

Homestead Day Nursery
NOTTINGHAM
Tel: 115 9652540

Honey Bee Day Nursery
20 Gotham Road, East Leake, LEICS
Tel: 01509 852666

Honey Pot Day Nursery
DERBY
Tel: 01332 830473

Honeypot Private Day Nursery
NOTTINGHAM
Tel: 0115 9314411

Hucknall Day Nursery
NOTTINGHAM
Tel: 0115 9680797

Humberston Day Nursery
LEICESTER
Tel: 0116 2202143

Humpty Dumpty Day Nurseries
STAFFS
Tel: 01543 473195

Jack & Jill Nursery
130 Green Lane, DERBY
Tel: 01332 382364
Quality childcare for 0-5 yrs.

Jack In The Box Day Nursery
DERBY
Tel: 01332 810025

Jigsaw Day Nursery
LEICESTER
Tel: 0116 2893083

John Clifford Nursery & Primary School
Nether Street, Beeston, NOTTINGHAM
Tel: 0115 9258057
Email: head@johnclifford.notts.sch.uk
Web: www.john-clifford-primary.co.uk
The school is a community school with a nursery unit, catering for children from 3-11 years.

Joint Responsibility
LEICESTER
Tel: 01509 621700

Just Learning Southwell
NOTTS
Tel: 01636 816606

Keepers Cottage Day Nursery
STAMFORD
Tel: 01780 721880

Kibworth Pre-School Nursery
LEICESTER
Tel: 0116 2793906

Kiddycare Day Nursery
LEICESTER
Tel: 0116 2680258

Kids Room Day Nursery
78 Uppingham Road, LEICESTER
Tel: 0116 2742835
Email: Kidsroom@btconnect.com
Web: www.btconnect.com

King Edward Park Nursery School
NOTTINGHAM
Tel: 0115 9150198

King Edward VII Day Nursery
LEICESTER
Tel: 01664 481506

Kingscliffe Day Nursery
LEICESTER
Tel: 01509 263325

Knighton Day Nursery
LEICESTER
Tel: 0116 2883030

Knossington Montessori Nursery School
LEICS
Tel: 01664 454808

La Petite Academy
DERBY
Tel: 01332 774413

Lansdowne Day Nursery
25 Lansdowne Road, Aylestone,
LEICESTER
Tel: 0116 2831586
Web: www.lansdownedaynursery.co.uk

Laurels Nursery School
LEICESTER
Tel: 0116 2693858

Leapfrog Day Nurseries
Second Avenue, Centrum 100
Burton On Trent, DERBYS
Tel: 01283 535000/510444

Leapfrog Day Nurseries
DERBY
Tel: 01332 518888

Leapfrog Day Nurseries
LEICESTER
Tel: 0116 2865566

Leapfrog Day Nurseries
DERBY
Tel: 01332 544321

Leapfrog Day Nursery Ltd
NOTTINGHAM
Tel: 0115 9264111
Email: info@leapfrogdaynurseries.co.uk
Web: www.leapfrogdaynurseries.co.uk

Leicester Early Years & Childcare
Leicester County Council, Room 144,
County Hall, Glenfield, LEICESTER
Tel: 0116 2658037

Leicester High School For Girls
LEICESTER
Tel: 0116 2705338
Web: www.leicesterhigh.co.uk

Leicester Montessori Day Nursery
LEICESTER
Tel: 0116 2702758

Leicester Montessori School
190 London Road, LEICESTER
Tel: 0116 2554442
Baby unit for 0-3 yrs.

Leicester Montessori School
LEICESTER
Tel: 0116 2554441

Leo's Day Nursery Ltd
NOTTINGHAM
Tel: 0115 9673229

Liberty House Day Nursery
LEICESTER
Tel: 0845 2300222

Lighthouse Day Nursery
LEICESTER
Tel: 0116 2886090

Liliput Montessori Day Nursery
LEICS
Tel: 01530 813913

Lilliput Montessori Day Nurseries
LEICESTER
Tel: 0116 2365353
Web: www.lilliputmontessoridaynurseries.co.uk

Little Acorns
DERBY
Tel: 01332 346088

Little Acorns Creche
LEICESTER
Tel: 01664 855353

Little Acorns Nursery
382 London Road, LEICESTER
Tel: 0116 2705086

Little Angels Day Nursery
LEICESTER
Tel: 01858 469708

Little Bears Day Nursery
1a First Avenue, Carlton, NOTTINGHAM
Tel: 0115 9404388
Web: www.littlebearsnursery.co.uk

Little Foxes
23 East Street, Oadby, LEICESTER
Tel: 0116 2718866

Little Jack Horners
DERBY
Tel: 01283 734030

Little Me Nurseries Ltd
Bramley House, 25 Main Street,
Foxton, Market Harborough, LEICESTER
Tel: 01858 540042
Email: littlemenursery@btinternet.com
Web: www.btinternet.com
Home from home 30 place Nursery.
Qualified staff and professional care.

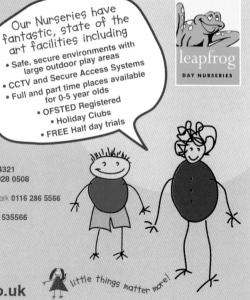
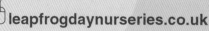

The Laurels Nursery School

The Laurels Nursery School is located on the Melton Road as you leave Queniborough for the A46 Syston bypass. The large Victorian house has been renovated completely to suit the needs of a modern, but very family oriented and friendly Nursery.

1514 Melton Road, Queniborough, Leicester LE7 3FN.
Tel: 01162 693858 Fax: 01162 698214

Little Foxes Day Nursery

Little Foxes Day Nursery is located on East Street in Oadby and stands adjacent to the large local shoppers car park. The building is a mid Victorian town house and is ideally suited to deliver a highly personalised standard of child care.

23 East Street, Oadby, Leicester LE2 5AF. Tel/Fax: 01162 718866

Little Acorns Nursery

Little Acorns Nursery is located at the heart of the Stoneygate area of Leicester, on the London Road travelling south out of Leicester towards Oadby. The building is a superb example of Edwardian architecture, retaining all of its warmth and character, and little has been changed to the house since it was converted to a Nursery in 1990.

382 London Road, Stoneygate, Leicester LE2 2PN.
Tel/Fax: 01162 705086

The Melton Mowbray Nursery School

The Melton Mowbray Nursery School is located on Dalby Road, virtually opposite the town swimming baths, in an early Victorian Grade 2 listed building. The Nursery began life as an example of a Melton Mowbray 'hunting lodge', but for much of the past 25 years has been used for more commercial purposes, including a vet's practise as well as a Nursery for the under 5's.

34 Dalby Road, Melton Mowbray, Leicester LE132 0BH.
Tel/Fax: 011664 569372

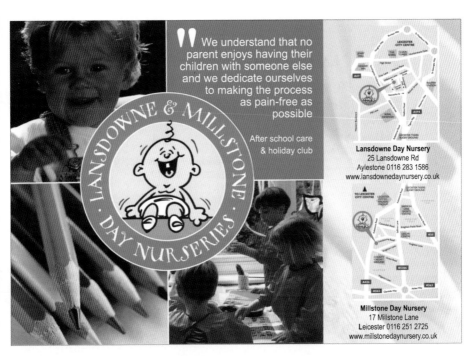

Little Monsters Day Nursery
Main Road, Anslow, Burton, DERBYS
Tel: 01283 815588

Little Oaks Nursery
NOTTINGHAM
Tel: 0115 9382022

Little Poppets
LEICESTER
Tel: 0800 5427561

Little Poppets
LEICESTER
Tel: 0800 5427561

Little Scholars
DERBY
Tel: 01332 760619

Little Stars Day Nursery
LEICESTER
Tel: 0116 2839991

Little Strawberry Nursery School
DERBYS
Tel: 01283 845554

Littlegates for Little People
NOTTS
Tel: 01636 626067

Longdale Nursery School
Longdale Lane, Ravenshead,
NOTTINGHAM
Tel: 01623 491919

Longfield Kindergarten
LEICESTER
Tel: 0116 2403721

Loughborough Campus Day Nursery
LEICESTER
Tel: 01509 234126

**Loughborough Children &
Family Centre**
LEICESTER
Tel: 01509 267360

Lutterworth Day Nursery Ltd
LEICESTER
Tel: 01455 556895

Lynton Childcare
LEICESTER
Tel: 01455 444110

**Mansfield Prep School &
Day Nursery**
Welbeck Road, Mansfield Woodhouse, NOTTS
Tel: 01623 420940

Market Bosworth Day Nursery
LEICESTER
Tel: 01455 290561

Markfield Day Nursery
LEICESTER
Tel: 01530 249789

Marlborough Day Nursery
LEICS
Tel: 01530 814051

Mary Poppins
DERBYS
Tel: 01332 510808

Mellors Nursery School
NOTTINGHAM
Tel: 0115 9151794

Nottinghamshire

eYp
dcp

Early Years
Development
and Childcare
Partnership

Leicestershire
County Council

Looking for Childcare?

Call now for FREE, impartial information and advice on childcare and children's services, including contact details of all OfSTED registered early years providers.

- childminders
- playgroups
- day nurseries
- out of school clubs
- holiday playschemes
- crèches

For Nottinghamshire call
0800
781 2168

For Leicestershire call
0116
265 6545

Merrivale Nursery School
NOTTINGHAM
Tel: 0115 9155767

Merry Go Round Childrens Nurseries
NOTTINGHAM
Tel: 0115 9677951

Mickleover Montessori Nursery School
DERBY
Tel: 0845 2300222

Millfield Nursery School
Millfield House, Tithby Road,
Cropwell Butler, NOTTINGHAM
Tel: 0115 9334085
Web: www.millfieldnurseryschool.co.uk

Millstone Day Nursery
17 Millstone Lane, LEICESTER
Tel: 0116 2512725
Web: www.millstonedaynursery.co.uk

Mother Hens Nursery
NOTTINGHAM
Tel: 01636 611603

Mountain Ash Day Nursery
150 Porchester Road, Mapperley,
NOTTINGHAM
Tel: 0115 9932915

Nanpantan Nursery School
LEICESTER
Tel: 01509 239203

New Walk Private Day Nursery
LEICESTER
Tel: 0116 2330423

Nightingale Nursery
DERBYS
Tel: 01332 875000

Nightingale Nursery
NOTTS
Tel: 0115 9731414

Nightingale Nursery
DERBY
Tel: 01332 811800

Nippers Nursery
LEICESTER
Tel: 0116 2535490

Noah's Ark Day Nursery
DERBYS
Tel: 01283 712112

Noah's Ark Play Group
NOTTINGHAM
Tel: 0115 9458553

Millfield Nursery School
(Private Day Nursery)

Tythby Road, Cropwell Butler,
Nottingham. NG12 3AJ
Telephone: 0115 933 4085
www.millfieldnurseryschool.co.uk

"Where children come to grow and learn, their happiness is our concern"

150 - 152 Porchester Road, Mapperley, Nottingham
Tel: 0115 9952915

North Notts Nurseries Ltd
NOTTS
Tel: 01623 660555

Nottingham Day Nurseries Associates
NOTTINGHAM
Tel: 0115 9856886

Nottingham Montessori School
NOTTINGHAM
Tel: 0845 2300222

Nunu Ltd
CHESHIRE
Tel: 0115 9463003
Web: www.nunu.uk.com

Nursery Network (UK) Ltd
DERBYS
Tel: 01283 569653

Nursery Network Ltd
DERBYS
Tel: 01283 569653
Web: www.nursery-network.co.uk

Oakdene House Day Nursery
NOTTINGHAM
Tel: 01623 420600

Oaktree Day Nursery
DERBYS
Tel: 01332 674326

Old Recton Nursery
LEICESTER
Tel: 01455 843929

Old School Nursery
Paget Street, Kibworth, LEICESTER
Tel: 0116 2796111

One-Lea House Nursery
LEICESTER
Tel: 01509 620909

Orchard Day Nurseries Ltd
DERBYS
Tel: 01332 728545

Orchard Day Nursery
DERBYS
Tel: 01332 370497

Orchard End Day Nursery
LEICESTER
Tel: 01455 615455

Orchard Nursery School
DERBYS
Tel: 01332 703204

Our Lady's Convent School
LEICS
Tel: 01509 263901

Paper Lace Day Nursery
NOTTINGHAM
Tel: 0115 9104680

Paper Moon Day Nurseries Group
10 Bonington Road, Mapperley, NOTTINGHAM
Tel: 0115 9691696

Paper Moon Day Nursery
Jasmine Road, Doddington Park LINCOLN
Tel: 01522 681681

Paper Moon Day Nursery
104 Boultham Park Road, LINCOLN
Tel: 01522 560562

Paper Moon Day Nursery
The Clock Tower, Compton Acres,
NOTTINGHAM
Tel: 0115 9811801

Paper Moon Day Nursery
Mansfield Road, Sutton In Ashfield, NOTTS

Paper Moon Day Nursery
Faraday Road, Lenton, NOTTINGHAM
Tel: 0115 9424800
Web: www.papermoondaynursery.co.uk

Parkside Nursery School
LEICESTER
Tel: 01509 213329

Parkview Day Nursery
LEICESTER
Tel: 0116 2734237

Pavillion Nursery and Pre-School
Warwick Road, Whetstone, LEICESTER
Tel: 0116 2864081
Ages from 8 wks-8 yrs.

Peapod Day Nursery
NOTTS
Tel: 01949 81522

Pebbles Nursery
LEICESTER
Tel: 0116 2712215
Web: www.pebblesnursery.co.uk

Pebble's Nursery
LEICESTER
Tel: 0116 2861992

Pebbles Nursery Knighton
LEICESTER
Tel: 0116 2706916

Pelham Day Nursery
NOTTS
Tel: 0115 9531474

Peter Pan Day Nursery
127 Station Road, Mickleover, DERBYS
Tel: 01332 512484
Private nursery for children aged 2-5 years.
Open 8.30 - 4pm Mon - Fri.

Pied Pipers
LEICESTER
Tel: 0116 2321312

Pinfold Gate Day Nursery
LEICESTER
Tel: 01509 269020

Play Days Nursery
1-3 Glenhills Boulevard, LEICESTER
Tel: 0116 2440727
Web: www.playdaysnursery.co.uk
Superior nursery care during a childs most
informative years.

Playroom Day Nursery
NOTTINGHAM
Tel: 0115 9811168

Poplars Nursery School
NOTTINGHAM
Tel: 0115 9676051

Poppies Day Nursery
NOTTS
Tel: 01636 626260

Pretty Windows Day Nursery
NOTTINGHAM
Tel: 0115 9881429

Priesthills Nursery
LEICESTER
Tel: 01455 614732

Progress House Day Nursery Ltd
96 Northampton Road, Market Harborough,
LEICESTER
Tel: 01858 431700

Puffins Day Nursery
LEICESTER
Tel: 01572 756714

Purpose Built Day Nursery
640 Melton Road, Thurmaston, LEICESTER
Tel: 0116 2640333
*As the name suggests, purposly built premises for
babies and children 0 -8 years open 7.30-6.30 Mon–Fri*

Quorn Grange Day Nursery
LEICESTER
Tel: 01509 412167

Ractcliffe-On Trent Day Nursery
NOTTINGHAM
Tel: 0115 9333133

Radcliffe-On-Trent Day Nursery
NOTTINGHAM
Tel: 0115 9333133

Radmoor Day Nursery
LEICESTER
Tel: 01509 618239

Rainbow Nursery
LEICESTER
Tel: 0116 2671331

Rhyme Times
DERBYS
Tel: 01332 770167

Richmond House Nursery School
LEICESTER
Tel: 01664 474217

River View Day Nurseries
LEICESTER
Tel: 0116 2554666

Robjohn Nursery
LEICESTER
Tel: 0116 2863717

Rothley Park Kindergarten
LEICESTER
Tel: 0116 2303888

Rowans Day Nursery
NOTTINGHAM
Tel: 0115 9166618

Ruddington Day Nursery
NOTTINGHAM
Tel: 0115 9848125

Scallywags Day Nursery
LEICESTER
Tel: 01572 723810

Scotts Wood Private Day Nursery
NOTTINGHAM
Tel: 0115 9812980

Serendipitys Day Nursery
NOTTINGHAM
Tel: 01949 836730
Web: www.serendipitysdaynursery.co.uk

Shanklin Day Nursery
LEICESTER
Tel: 0116 2704603

Shaping Futures Day Nurseries
NOTTINGHAM
Tel: 01636 613829

Silver Trees Day Nursery
DERBYS
Tel: 01332 366663

Silvertrees Day Nursery
NOTTINGHAM
Tel: 0115 9732311
Web: www.silvertrees-notts.co.uk

Small World Day Nursery
NOTTINGHAM
Tel: 0115 9553703

Small World Nursery
LEICESTER
Tel: 01509 262922

Small World Private Day Nursery
DERBYS
Tel: 01332 751869

Smarties Day Nursery
LEICESTER
Tel: 0116 2861407

Smiles Daycare Ltd
192 Poplar Street, NOTTINGHAM
Tel: 0115 9243003

Smisby Day Nursery
LEICS
Tel: 01530 416279

Southfields Pre-School
NOTTINGHAM
Tel: 01949 20123

St Josephs Nursery
NOTTINGHAM
Tel: 0115 9418356
Web: www.st-josephs.nottingham.school.uk

St Lawrence Pre-School & Club 11
NOTTINGHAM
Tel: 0115 9721405

St. Bernards Private Day Nursery
LEICESTER
Tel: 01455 635456

St. George Nursery School
LEICESTER
Tel: 0116 2517755

St. Georges Nursery School
LEICESTER
Tel: 0116 2716161

St. George's Nursery School
LEICESTER
Tel: 0116 2833383

St. Marys Montessori Day Nursery
LEICESTER
Tel: 01455 554034

Stanhope Hosue Day Nursery Ltd
LEICESTER
Tel: 0116 2554277

Station House Day Nursery
NOTTINGHAM
Tel: 0115 9259898

Staunton Montessori Nursery School
NOTTINGHAM
Tel: 01400 282860
Email: www.st-m.com

Stepping Stones Day Nursery
42-44 Attenborough Lane,
Beeston, NOTTINGHAM
Tel: 0115 9223144

Stepping Stones Day Nursery Ltd
The Arboretum, NOTTINGHAM
Tel: 0115 9101162
Web: www.steppingstonesltd.com
Quailty day nursery and childcare.

Stepping Stones Nursery
2 Storer Road, Loughborough LEICESTER
Tel: 01509 217275

Stockhill Lane Day Nursery
NOTTINGHAM
Tel: 0115 9422320

Stoneygate College & Kindergarten
LEICESTER
Tel: 0116 2707414

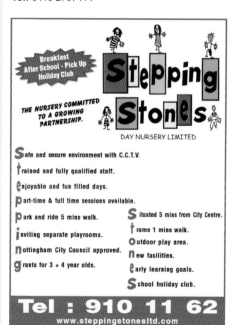

Stork Day Nursery
LEICESTER
Tel: 01455 635656

Sunshine Corner Day Nursery
NOTTINGHAM
Tel: 0115 8402073

Sunshine Day Nursery
DERBYS
Tel: 01283 563279

Sunshine Nursery
LEICESTER
Tel: 0800 5427561

T.A.R.D.I.S Nursery
65-67 Radford Road, Hyson Green
NOTTINGHAM
Tel: 0115 9117368
A safe stimulating environment for your children.
OFSTED registered. Fully qualified staff.

Tangent House Day Nursery
LEICESTER
Tel: 0116 2640333

The Carlton Day Nurseries

Full day-care for children aged 0-8 years.
with sites at;

Allestree
01332 366223

Hilton
01283 730730

Sinfin
01332 766636

THE CARLTON

Tea Pots Day Nursery
LEICESTER
Tel: 01455 286688

Teddies Nurseries
TWICKENHAM
Tel: 0800 9803801

Tender Loving Childcare Ltd
NOTTINGHAM
Tel: 0115 9229117

The Ark Nursery
NOTTINGHAM
Tel: 0115 9624594

The Awsworth School House Day Nursery
NOTTINGHAM
Tel: 0115 9444114
Web: www.kiddiesfirst.co.uk

The Carlton Day Nursery
Maxwell Avenue, Allestree, DERBY
Tel: 01332 366223
Full day-care for children aged 1-8 yrs.

The Carlton Day Nursery
Hilton
Tel: 01283 730730
Full day-care for children aged 0-8 yrs.

The Carlton Day Nursery
Sinfin, DERBY
Tel: 01332 766636
Full day-care for children 0-8 yrs.

The Castle Garden Private Day Nursery
DERBY
Tel: 01332 841844

The Childcare Corporation
NOTTINGHAM
Tel: 0115 9859333

The Childrens House
NOTTINGHAM
Tel: 01636 814738

The Clockhouse Pre School Centre
NOTTINGHAM
Tel: 0115 9121300

The Cottage
DERBY
Tel: 01332 346500

The Cottage Private Day Nursery
DERBY
Tel: 01332 346500

The Cottage Private Day Nursey
NOTTS
Tel: 01773 715726
Email: heanor@cottagenurseries.co.uk
Web: www.cottagenurseries.co.uk

The Dolls House
LEICESTER
Tel: 0116 2236357

The Firs Day Nursery
DERBYS
Tel: 01283 564734

The Gooseberry Bush
NOTTINGHAM
Tel: 0115 9822220

The Grange Nursery School
LEICESTER
Tel: 0116 2707820

The Honey Bee Day Nursery
20 Gotham Road, East Leake,
Loughborough, LEICESTER
Tel: 01509 852666

The Honey Pots Day Nursery
DERBY
Tel: 01283 539200

The Lanes Private Day Nursery
NOTTS
Tel: 0115 9440810

The Laurels
1514 Melton Road, Queniborough LEICESTER
Tel: 0116 2693858

The Market Harborough Nursery School
LEICESTER
Tel: 01858 464172

The Melton Mowbray Nursery School
34 Dalby Road, Melton Mowbray, LEICESTER
Tel: 01664 569372

The Mulberry Bush Nursery
LEICESTER
Tel: 0116 2571774

The Mulberry Bush Nursery School
DERBYS
Tel: 01335 342474

The Mulberry Bush Nursery School
DERBY
Tel: 01332 344800

The Old Co-Operative Day Nursery Ltd
7/9 Wallace Street, Gotham NOTTS
Tel: 0115 9830003

The Old Fire Station
NOTTS
Tel: 01623 490222

The Old Forge Day Nursery
DERBYS
Tel: 01283 701533

The Orchard Day Nursery
NOTTINGHAM
Tel: 0115 9227955

The Pavilion Pre-School & Day Nursery
LEICESTER
Tel: **0116 2864081**

The Pines
DERBYS
Tel: 0115 9305550

The Rocking Horse Nursery
NOTTS
Tel: 0115 9305240

The Three Bears Nursery School
LEICESTER
Tel: 0116 2461122

The Village Nursery
NOTTINGHAM
Tel: 0115 9254027

The Village Private Day Nursery
DERBYS
Tel: 01332 669686

The White House Day Nursery
LOUGHBORUGH
Tel: 01509 505555

The Woodlands Private Day Nursery
DERBYS
Tel: 01332 346878

The Young Ones Day Nursery
443 Derby Road, NOTTINGHAM
Tel: 0115 9790988

Three Bears Nursery School
LEICESTER
Tel: 0116 2461122

Tinkerbell's Day Nursery
LEICESTER
Tel: 01509 217271

Tiny Gems Nursery
LEICESTER
Tel: 0116 2760504

Tiny Steps Day Nursery
NOTTINGHAM
Tel: 0115 9259111

Tiny Tots Pre-School
LEICESTER
Tel: 0116 2215705

Tiny Tots Private Day Nursery
DERBYS
Tel: 01332 572387

Toddlers Nursery School
LEICESTER
Tel: 0116 2321445

Toddlers University
NOTTS
Tel: 0115 9444294

Tom Thumb Nursery
DERBYS
Tel: 01283 840170

Topsham House Day Nursery
16 Peckleton Lane, Desford, LEICESTER
Tel: 01455 828885
Email: admin@topshamhouse.co.uk
Web: www.topshamhouse.co.uk
Quality day nursery, qualified caring staff.
Stimulating enviroment with pre school.

Topspinney Nursery School
NOTTINGHAM
Tel: 0115 9262096

Tots World
NOTTINGHAM
Tel: 0845 6443912

Toybox Private Day Nursery
Derby College, Pride Parkway
Pride Park, DERBY
Tel: 01332 756751

Tree Tops Childrens Day Nursery
DERBYS
Tel: 01335 342712

Treetops Day Nursery
NOTTINGHAM
Tel: 0115 9166250

Trent Fields Kindergarton & Preparatory
21 Trent Boulevard, West Bridgford,
NOTTINGHAM
Tel: 0115 9821685

Send info.True Care Day Nursery
LEICESTER
Tel: 0116 2786040

Unit Hospital Day Nursery
NOTTINGHAM
Tel: 0115 9420978

Up-Starts Nursery
LEICESTER
Tel: 01572 821210

Valmarys Childrens Centre
NOTTINGHAM
Tel: 0115 9604259

Vernon Park Day Nursery
NOTTINGHAM
Tel: 0115 9782274

Vicar Water Day Nursery
NOTTS
Tel: 01623 660555

West Point House Day Nursery
ILKESTON
Tel: 0115 932 5718

Westcotes Day Nursery
LEICESTER
Tel: 0116 2546413

Westleigh Nursery
LEICESTER
Tel: 0116 2554152

Westwards Nursery School
LEICESTER
Tel: 01509 214551

Westways at Uppingham School
LEICESTER
Tel: 01572 822262

Where Children Come First
NOTTINGHAM
Tel: 0115 9333133

White House Day Nursery
55 Forest Street, Shepshed,
Loughborough, LEICESTER
Tel: 01509 505555
Web: www.whitehousedaynursery.co.uk
Nursery and out of school care from 0-13 years.
7am - 6pm Mon-Fri.

Whitehouse Childrens Nurseries
DERBYS
Tel: 01332 666414

Whitehouse Day Nursery
DERBYS
Tel: 01332 661922

Whitehouse Day Nursery
NOTTINGHAM
Tel: 0115 9810119

Whitwick Day Nursery
LEICS
Tel: 01530 830499

Windmill Lane Day Nursery
DERBYS
Tel: 01335 300623

Windsor House Private Day Nursery
LEICESTER
Tel: 0116 2682550

Wingfiled Day Nursery
140 Westcotes Drive, LEICESTER
Tel: 0116 2541239

Wishing Well Day Nurseries
2 Oakfields Road, West Bridgford, NOTTINGHAM
Tel: 0115 9142233

Wollaton Village Day Nurseries
NOTTS
Tel: 01773 711721

Woodend Private Day Nursery
DERBYS
Tel: 01283 704555

Woodlands Day Nursery
1 Park Road, Birstall, LEICESTER
Tel: 0116 2675427

Woodlands Private Day Nursery
1 Gibfield Lane, Belper, DERBYS
Tel: 01773 882423

Woodlands Private Day Nursery
95 Shardlow Road, Alvaston, DERBY
Tel: 01332 861731

Woodlands Private Day Nursery
194 Duffield Road, DERBYS
Tel: 01332 346878

Woodthorpe Day Nursery
NOTTINGHAM
Tel: 0115 9620415

Woodville Day Nursery
DERBYS
Tel: 01283 552277

Yellow Brick Road Nursery
2 Stonehill Road, DERBY
Tel: 01332 600640
Quality childcare from 3 mths - 13 yrs. Includes
BSC, ASC and holiday club.

MONTESSORI GROUP

Baby Units, Nurseries and Pre-Schools

- Children from 6 weeks to 11 years
- Montessori Education
- Dedicated and experienced Nursery Nurses and Teachers
- Full or part time sessions from 7.30am to 6pm
- Open 51 weeks of the year
- After school and holiday clubs

Nottingham Montessori School
2 The Connery, Hucknall

Mickleover Montessori School
Staker Lane, Mickleover

Leicester Montessori School

137 Loughborough Rd,
Leicester

291 Liberty Road,
Leicester

190 London Road,
Leicester

279 London Road,
Leicester

1096 Melton Road,
Syston,
Leicester

84 Station Road,
Wigston,
Leicester

Preparatory, Grammar and Sixth Form College also in Leicester

www.montessorigroup.com

For more information or to visit please call our admissions department

0116 255 4441

Putting your child first and foremost

The search for the right nursery questionnaire - Baby room: birth too walk

Questions	tick/cross	comments
Were we welcome in the nursery		
Did the staff interact with my child?		
Were the staff interacting well with other children?		
Were the staff cheerful & helpful?		
Was the room stimulating & bright?		
Did the children in the room appear happy & well cared for?		
Were activities in the room age appropriate?		
What was the security like?		
Was the nursery safe & clean?		
What were the staff qualifications?		
What is staff turn over like?		
What is the ability/age grouping in my child's room?		
What is the staff to child ratios in my child's room?		
What development records will be kept on my child?		
Are the staff aware of the prevention of S.I.D. (cot death prevention)?		
What are the sleeping arrangements like for babies?		
Are the babies given lots of loves and cuddles?		
Is the food prepared fresh/ special requirements catered for ?		
Do the children go out for walks/ nursery trips?		
Is positive behaviour encouraged?		
Do they target realistic goals of learning for the children?		
Are staff first aid qualified?		
How long is the waiting list?		
How much is a place?		
What are the hours of opening?		
Can I make build up visits?		
Did my baby enjoy the environment?		
Did we like the overall feel of the nursery?		
From1-20 how did this baby room suit your family's needs?		

The search for the right nursery questionnaire - Pre-school room 3: to 5 years

Questions	tick/cross	comments
Were we welcome in the nursery		
Did the staff interact with my child?		
Were the staff interacting well with other children?		
Were the staff cheerful & helpful?		
Was the room stimulating & bright?		
Did the children in the room appear happy & well cared for?		
Were activities in the room age appropriate?		
Did the room plans reflect an interesting & varied day?		
What was the security like?		
Was the nursery safe & clean?		
What were the staff qualifications?		
What is staff turn over like?		
What is the ability/age grouping in my child's room?		
What are the ratios in my child's room?		
What development records will be kept on my child?		
Is there a computer available for children's use?		
Were the early years goals as set by the government in place?		
Is the nursery Ofsted available to view?		
Are the children given lots of loves and cuddles?		
Is my child allowed his/her comforts?		
Is the food prepared fresh/ special requirements catered for?		
Do the children go out for walks/ nursery trips?		
Is positive behaviour encouraged?		
How are children made aware of achievements?		
Do you liase with the local feeder school?		
Are staff first aid qualified?		
How long is the waiting list?		
How much is a place?		
What are the hours of opening?		
Can I make build up visits?		
Did my Child enjoy the environment?		
Did we like the overall feel of the nursery?		
From1-20 how did this Pre-school room suit your family's needs?		

Babes 2 Tots
LEICESTER
Tel: 01530 564446

Baby Dotty Box
9 Deepdale Close, Gamston, NOTTINGHAM
Tel: 0115 9812504

Baby Love
LEICESTER
Tel: 0116 2832170

Baby Planet
LEICESTER
Tel: 0116 2556222

Babyquip
LEICESTER
Tel: 0116 2740573

Bambino Baby and Nursery Goods
52 Rectory Road, West Bridgford,
NOTTINGHAM
Tel: 0115 9141434
Email: karen@bambino.org.uk
Web: www.bambino.org.uk
*Stockists of Mamas & Papas, Bugaboo,
Maclaren and many more.*

Brave Little Soldiers
LEICESTER
Tel: 0116 2719016

Bristols Early Days
61 Outram Street, Sutton-In-Ashfield,
NOTTS
Tel: 01623 554227
Web: www.bristolsearlydays.co.uk

Children's Choice
17 Bridge Street, Belper
DERBYS
Tel: 01773 825865
*Speacialists in schoolwear.Official scout's
and guide's shop, children's fashions from
newborn to teens. Nursery equipment .
Everything for need for your baby!*

Cot Beds Direct
6 Park Lane, Castle Donington
DERBYS
Tel: 01332 812825
*Only official reseller of Tutti Bambini
nursery furniture in the East Midlands*

Diddyland
906 Woodboorough Road, Mapperley,
NOTTINGHAM
Tel: 0115 9623000
Web: www.diddyland.co.uk
*Nursery goods and furniture.
Personal ordering service.*

Early Times
DERBYS
Tel: 01332 541561

First Steps
LEICESTER
Tel: 01858 462123

Jaq-B-Nimble
LEICESTER
Tel: 0116 2693356

Jellyrolls Nursery
35 Silver Street,
LEICESTER
Tel: 0116 2623503

Nurserygoods.com
LEICESTER
Tel: 01276 686161

Prams 'N' Things
108 St. Marys Road,
Market Harborough,
LEICESTER
Tel: 01858 433775
*Stockists of Mamas and Papas,
Silvercross, Jane, Brittax, bebe
Car, Baby Style and many more!*

The new concept for bathing and relaxing babies up to 6 months.

For many months inside your womb your baby has enjoyed a warm, safe and secure environment. The sudden change can be very traumatic and most babies need time to adjust to their new surroundings.

The Original Tummy Tub® was designed in the Netherlands with the help and cooperation of Paediatricians and midwives, to ease the transition into the outside world. The unique design of Tummy Tub ensures that your baby will naturally adopt the foetal position giving a reassuring feeling and it is amazing to see how quickly they calm and relax. (Many babies do not like lying on their backs and often panic resulting in tears, this can be very distressing for both parent and baby). The benefits are acknowledged in homes and maternity hospitals throughout Europe where doctors, midwives and health visitors endorse it. It is currently used by more than 125 maternity hospitals in the UK.

The Original Tummy Tub® makes bath time enjoyable from birth and gives reassurance to babies at any time of the day or night, when stressed. Babies can be immersed up to shoulder level safely and remain warmer for longer.

Parents and carers also benefit from using the Original Tummy Tub®, stress free bathing, easy handling, lightweight even when full, ergonomic hand grips and a wide rim to support the parents' arms all help to make bath time easy. An anti-skid base offers extra safety. All possible safety features have been built into the Original Tummy Tub®.

It is also ideal for use when away for a night, weekend or even on a holiday, ensuring that baby does not have to undergo any stressful changes wherever bath time is carried out.

The Original Tummy Tub® is especially recommended for premature babies and will help unsettled babies calm and sleep, as well as being excellent for colicky babies. The Tummy Tub has been available in the UK for almost 10 years.

Made from a recyclable polypropylene, the Original Tummy Tub® is easy to clean and conforms to CE Certification 93/42 EWG Medical product law regulations, it also has the Rheinland TUV safety certificate/assessed by BSI. Beware of cheap imitations.

The Tummy Tub® costs £19.99 inc postage and packing and is available from CN Sales & Marketing Ltd or from retailers throughout the UK.

CN Sales & Marketing Ltd, UK distributors for Tummy Tub® can be found at www.tummytub.co.uk and can be contacted by phone on 01635 255725 or by email at sales@tummytub.co.uk The website has an instructional video.

Jo Jo Maman Bebe
Distribution House, Oxwich Road,
Newport, SOUTH WALES
Tel: 0870 241 0560
Web: www.jojomamanbebe.co.uk
Extremely Stylish maternity wear at
reasonable prices, plusl underwear,
nursery goods and children's clothing.

John Lewis
NOTTINGHAM
Tel: 0115 9418282

Kids 'N' Co
LEICESTER
Tel: 0116 2303212

Kinder Garden
LEICESTER
Tel: 01509 234532

Le Carrousel
25 Hockley, NOTTINGHAM
Tel: 0115 9505169
Web: www.lecarrousel.co.uk
Nursery Retailer of the year 2004.

Little Monsters
LEICESTER
Tel: 0116 2674925

Little Used
DERBY
Tel: 01332 513144

Magic Roundabout
DERBYS
Tel: 01335 346663

Mothercare plc
LEICESTER
Tel: 01923 210 210

Mothercare Uk Ltd
BURTON ON TRENT
Tel: 01283 567 472

Mothercare Uk Ltd
DERBYS
Tel: 01332 280570

Mothercare Uk Ltd
NOTTS
Tel: 01636 701695

Mothercare UK Ltd
LEICESTER
Tel: 0116 2620768

Mothercare World
DERBYS
Tel: 01332 280570

Mothercare World
DERBYS
Tel: 01332 280750

Mum's The Word
LEICESTER
Tel: 01455 550789

Nappies-Nature Babies
LEICESTER
Tel: 01509 621879
Web: www.naturebabies.co.uk

Nappy Hopper Nappy Laundering Service
LINCOLN
Tel: 01522 684495
Web: www.nappyhopper.co.uk

R.S.B. Associates
LEICESTER
Tel: 01509 881300

Scopp 'A' Diddle
LEICESTER
Tel: 0116 2203207

Small World Interiors
36 Francis Street, Stoneygate,
LEICESTER
Tel: 0116 2704466
Web: www.smallworldinteriors.com
For children of all ages-interiors, gifts and toys.

Swingers & Rockers
GWYNEDD
Tel: 01758 780305
Web: www.cradles.co.uk

Stork Talk Superstore
Birkdale Close, Manners Road
Industrial Estate, DERBYS
Tel: 0115 9306700
Web: www.chiccomailorder.co.uk

The Whole Kaboodle
DERBYS
Tel: 01773 828000

Tummy Tubs
CN Sales and Marketing,
P O Box 5562,
NEWBURY, Berks
Tel: 01635 255725
Web: www.tummytub.co.uk

Whizzy Wheels
69 Queens Road,
Clarendon Park,
LEICESTER, LE2 1TT
Tel: 0116 2702888
Email: info@whizzywheels.co.uk
Web: www.whizzywheels.co.uk
Former mid-wife and neo-natal nurse owner. Bespoke service tailored to customer requirements. Free impartial advice.

le carrousel

Nottingham's Premier Pram & Nursery Store

Emmaljunga

**Voted Nursery Retailer of the year 2004/05
by the British Association of Nursery Pram Retailers**

*We are proud to represent emmaljunga,
Europes oldest and most probably modern pram factory.*
Susan Carnill Director

Open Tuesday - Saturday 10am - 5pm
25 Hockley, Nottingham, NG1 1FH
Tel: 0115 950 5169 • Fax: 0115 950 6107
email: info@lecarrousel.co.uk • www.lecarrousel.co.uk

*Also stockists of Jane • silver cross • mountain buggy • babystyle • britax
• chicco • bebe • confort • maclaren • bebecar • eichorn • instep • stokke
• baby bjorn • bambino mio • bug a boo*

*Extensive second floor showroom with furniture sets and nursery decor, to many to mention.
Hire repair and delivery service available.*

Le Carrousel Our World Revolves around You and Your little one.

Dignity Fairtrade
NOTTINGHAM
Tel: 07790 329 685

Fresh Food Company
Tel: 0208 749 8778
Web: www.freshfood.co.uk

Pots for Tots
Web: www.potsfortots.co.uk

The Organic Baby Food Company
Tel: 01666 505 616
Web: www.tetbury.com/baby

The Tea and Coffee Plant
Tel: 0207 221 8137
Web: www.coffee.uk.com

www.bathorganicbabyfood.co.uk
Tel: 01761 239 300

www.hipp.co.uk
Tel: 01635 528 250

Osteopathy

A. Fishie Osteopaths
NOTTINGHAM
Tel: 0115 9625 888

Back to Health
LEICESTER
Tel: 0116 282 6142

Backsetc
LEICESTER
Tel: 0116 291 2807

Beeston Natural Therapy Centre
NOTTINGHAM
Tel: 0115 9431 204

Christopher Stapleton
NOTTINGHAM
Tel: 0115 948 4141

Derby Osteopathic Centre
DERBY
Tel: 01332 383951

Graham Scarr
NOTTINGHAM
Tel: 0115 949 1753

Harborough Osteopathis Clinic
MARKET HARBOROUGH
Tel: 01858 410071

James Booth
NOTTINGHAM
Tel: 0115 923 2425

Laycock & Pollock
NEWARK
Tel: 01636 613334

Maple House Clinic
EASTWOOD
Tel: 01773 530268

Newark Osteopathy Clinic
NEWARK
Tel: 01636 611644

Richard H Edmunds
BURTON
Tel: 01283 543398

Richard Hepple
NOTTINGHAM
Tel: 0115 925 8055

The Derby Osteopathic Practice
DERBY
Tel: 01332 371184

Wigston Osteopathic Clininc
LEICESTER
Tel: 0116 257 1234

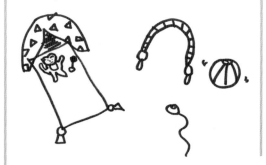

Love YOUR body and YOUR baby

During the pregnancy your body will experience many changes and as your "bump" grows so your posture will have to alter to accommodate this. Sometimes as the posture alters you can experience aches and pains. Many mums-to-be complain of back pain and sciatic pain (pain down into their legs) which can be very debilitating. Usually the aches and pains of pregnancy respond well to the gentle manipulation and soft tissue treatment of a qualified Osteopath, and this will then in turn make labour easier.

Labour itself can be tiring and sometimes involves intervention from the hospital that can leave you achy and feeling a little low. Your osteopath will also be able to help you at this time to return to normal as quickly as possible and can liase with GPs or health visitors if needed. Babies themselves whether they are born naturally or by caesarean go through quite a stressful and sometimes tramatic time. Some do very well and recover without any help, others may show symptoms of colic, sleeplessness or irritability and as any new mum knows it makes life very hard work to have a grizzly baby that will not settle!

Often babies that have feeding problems respond really well to gentle treatment and frequent feeding or poor weight gain can sometimes mean that baby is taking in too much air as they feed and feeling full when actually they are not. All osteopaths are trained to look after pregnant mums and babies but there are osteopaths that have undergone extra training in the care of mothers and babies and these have the letters DPO after their name. Osteopaths are legally required to be registered with a governing body known as the GOsC and can be found listed in the yellow pages.

Osteopathic treatment of babies is very very gentle and cannot harm your baby, if you would like advice most osteopaths are happy to answer any queries via the telephone before you book your appointments. Never be afraid to ask!!!

For further details contact the GOsC on 020 7357 6655 or visit:www.osteopathy.org.uk

Art Leisure
21 Balmoral Road, Colwick, NOTTINGHAM
Tel: 0115 9611567

Cotgrave Leisure Centre
Woodview, Cotgrave NOTTINGHAM
Tel: 0115 9892916

Crazy Crocodiles
Abbey Street, Ilkeston, DERBYS
Tel: 0115 9441 555
All year round indoor adventure play centre for children 0 -10 yrs.

Denby Pottery Visitor Centre
on B6179, off A38, 2 miles south of Ripley
Denby, DERBYS
Tel: 01773 740700
Lot's of activities & entertainment, for children, during school holidays

Freddy's Play Kingdom
50 Nottingham Road, Spondon, DERBY
Tel: 01332 662322
Childrens activity play and play centre. Discos, parties catered for-cafeteria serving food and drink.

Funky Pots
278/280 Huntington Street,
NOTTIGNHAM
Tel: 0115 9298025
Email: info@funkypots.co.uk
Web: www.info@funkypots.co.uk

Glitzy Girls Parties
19 Lincoln Drive, Mansfield, NOTTS
Tel: 01623 633963
Web: www.glitzygirls.co.uk

Its My Party
NOTTINGHAM
Tel: 07974 109841

Jolly Jingles Funtime
45 Co-operative Street, Long Eaton,
NOTTINGHAM
Tel: 0845 0090848
Email: clown@jollyjingles.co.uk
Web: www.jollyjingles.co.uk

Kiddy Kastle's
LEICESTER
Tel: 0116 2592842

Louby Lou
NOTTINGHAM
Tel: 0115 9130979
Face painting, hair braiding, balloon modeling for

Magic Moments Parties & Catering
NOTTINGHAM
Tel: 0115 9314309

Paint a Pot,
115 High Road, Beeston, NOTTINGHAM
Tel: 0115 9228029
A different and fun party for children of all ages at Paint a Pot. Parties are 1 1/2 hours long.

Paint a Pot
Markeaton Park Craft Village,
Markeaton Park, DERBY
Tel: 01332 202652
A different and fun party for children of all ages at Paint a Pot. Parties are 11/2 hours long.

Party Angels
DERBYS
Tel: 07940 113 207

Planet Happy
Heague Road Ind Estate, Ripley, DERBYS
Tel: 01773 748600

Playland
Unit 1a Botany Commercial Park,
Botany Avenue, Mansfield, NOTTS
Tel: 01623 654712
Indoor Play Centre, large under 3 area, tots 2-10 yrs, parties and food available.

Rushcliffe Arena
Rugby Road, West Bridgford, NOTTINGHAM
Tel: 0115 9814027
Childrens indoor soft play area and after school club, great venue for children's parties.

Scalliwags
Hilltop Mill, 49 Church Street,
Earl Shilton, LEICESTER
Tel: 01455 840536

St Leonards Riding School
Nottingham Road, Toton, NOTTINGHAM
Tel: 0115 9732753

Party Shops

The Party Shop
DERBYS
Tel: 01332 574751

Personal Trainers

4Life
NOTTINGHAM
Tel: 0115 9229791

Andrea Bell Personal Trainer
2 Moor Furlong, Stretton, BURTON ON TRENT
Tel: 01283 563708
Email: mail@abell40.fsnet.co.uk
Web: www.abell40
Improve your fitness level and change the shape of your body in the comfort of your own home. Advice on diet and calorie consumption. Also full training programmes available for pre-natal and post-natal requirements.

One 2 One Personal Fitness
Commercial Square, LEICESTER
Tel: 0116 2626611
Private fully equipped gym, all levels welcome. Strictly one to one, car parking and showers available.

Pure Personal Training
10 Kenrick Road, Mapperley, NOTTINGHAM
Tel: 07968 836549
Email: puretraining@aol.com

Exercise and Pregnancy

Exercising whilst pregnant is something which still causes confusion; is it safe to exercise or not? The answer is definitely yes, as long as you follow a common sense approach and exercise safely.

The level of exercise will depend largely upon your pre-pregnancy fitness. This is a time to maintain your fitness levels, not try to make dramatic improvements. You shouldn't attempt to run your first marathon or take up scuba diving but recent research has shown that moderate, regulated exercise is beneficial for both mother and baby.

Although exercise may be the last thing on your mind, a little regular exercise can help you cope with all the stages of pregnancy. As exercise promotes muscle tone, strength and endurance you'll find it easier to deal with the additional weight gained during pregnancy. Your cardiovascular system (your heart and lungs) will improve with regular exercise so you won't tire as easily and be better prepared for labour. Exercise will improve your posture, especially important in the later stages and can relieve back and muscle soreness. Your circulation will improve, helping with varicose veins. Exercise can also strengthen your abdominal and pelvic floor muscles safely which will help in your recovery after the birth.

A regular exercise programme will minimise weight gain, help you feel in control of your ever changing body and make getting back into shape after the baby is born much easier.

This is a stressful and exciting time, a period of change, not only physically but mentally and exercise can help to relax you, releasing endorphins: the body's natural painkillers.

Whatever your fitness level consult your doctor before exercising whilst pregnant and take the advice of a qualified and experienced fitness professional to ensure that you are exercising safely. At Pure Personal Training we are a small, select team with a diverse range of knowledge; all of our Personal Trainers are specialists in pre-and post-natal fitness.

At Pure we have a relaxed and professional approach with the emphasis on individually tailoring your sessions to make sure they are enjoyable, but most of all safe for you and your baby.

By being able to cope with the stresses and strains of pregnancy most mothers find the whole experience more rewarding – and of course your baby also directly benefits from your physical good health.

Allestree Foto Color
DERBY
Tel: 01332 556 318

Chapel Studio
1 Newbridge Road, Ambergate, DERBYSHIRE
Tel: 01773 852277
Web: www.chapelstudiouk.com
Wedding and portrait photography with style".
Lifestyle family portraits from birth onwards.
"Watch me grow" portraits."

Double Image Photography
21 Chilwell Road, Beeston, NOTTINGHAM
Tel: 0115 9252725
Email: info@doubleimagaephotography.co.uk
Web: www.doubleimagaephotography.co.uk
Studio portraits in a relaxed, friendly atmosphere.
Baby packages available.

Fluck Photography
32-40 Carrington Street, NOTTINGHAM
Tel: 0115 8410153

Fotomargo Ltd
NOTTINGHAM
Tel: 0115 9822032

Inspirations Photography
3 Portland Arcade, King Street,
SOUTHWELL, Notts
Tel: 01636 813766
Web: www.inspirationsofsouthwell.co.uk
Contemporary lifestyle portrait and wedding
photography.

Louise Kelham Photography
LEICESTER
Tel: 0116 2675019

Michael Clarke Photography and Design
122 Hoe View Road, Cropwell Bishop,
NOTTINGHAM
Tel: 0115 9890532
Email: mac.photos@totalise.co.uk
Web: www.mcpd.net
See advert on page 13

Monochrome Studio
517 Woodborough Road, Mapperley,
NOTTINGHAM
Tel: 0115 9606755
Web: www.monochromestudio.co.uk
Contemporary black & white photography-award
winning images.

Peter Horton
36 Amber Road, Allestree, DERBY

Photography by Tanya
463 Tamworth Road
Long Eaton, NOTTINGHAM
Tel: 0115 9730559
Web: www.photographybytanya.co.uk

Picture House Centre
Photography Ltd
LEICESTER
Tel: 0116 2555282

FLUK

PHOTOGRAPHY & VIDEO
The Award Winning Image Makers

The first thing you notice when you walk into the FLUK Studios in Nottingham is how relaxed you feel. The pictures lining the walls depict no forced smiles, just people at their best.

Putting people at ease has been one of the reasons why so many clients arrive at the FLUK Studios by recommendation.

Tel: 0115 8410153 . WWW.FLUKSTUDIOS.COM
32 - 40 Carrington St, Nottingham NG1 7FG

FLUK

PHOTOGRAPHY & VIDEO

So how do you put an infant at ease? How do you take that shot that, will take pride of place on a parents wall and grandma's mantelpiece?

Photographer and proprietor Ursula Kelly: "There is a great responsibility when photographing children. They grow so fast and change so much from week to week and month to month. So it's important to get it right first time. One should always work with the parents to put the children at ease.

A two year old can't always be reasoned with but they can be entertained and when they are happy you are more likely to get pictures during their grumpy moments too and you will be surprised how much character comes out in the final image. Kids get bored and kids get tired. Kids start school and kids change shape.

We can't stop these changes but we can remember them. I like to think that in twenty years time it's the pictures that I took that get passed around or pointed out to the new boyfriend or girlfriend! I hope that parents will use them as an accurate reminder of the times that have passed yet remembered with fondness."

Portraits at Home
27 Welling Lane, Edwalton, NOTTS
Tel: 0115 9231537

Profiles
168 Derby Road, Stapleford,
NOTTINGHAM
Tel: 0115 9394998

Shoot the Kids
Matlock, DERBYS
Tel: 01629 580780
Email: andrew@shoot-the-kids.co.uk
Web: www.shoot-the-kids.co.uk

Stu Williamson
Tel: 01858 469544
Web: www.stuwilliamson.com

Venture Nottingham
NOTTINGHAM
Tel: 01159 599999

Wisteria House Photographics
ARNOLD
Tel: 0115 9260742

Places of Interest

Cadbury World
Tel: 0121 200 2700

Green's Windmill & Science Centre
Windmill lane, Sneinton, Nottingham
Tel: 0115 915 6878
Web: www.greensmill.org.uk
Open Wed – Sun, Free
Once home to George Green who made important
discoveries about electricity, light and magnetism.
Tour the windmill to see grain turn into flour, then
test your mind with science-interactives. Plus
under fives area.

Legoland
Tel: 08705 040404
Web: www.legoland.co.uk

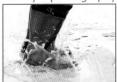

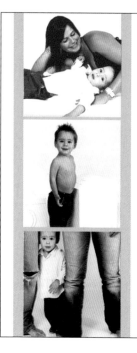

Photography by

Tanya.

Award Winning Photographer

463 Tamworth Road, Long Eaton,
Nottingham NG10 3GR.
Tel: 0115 973 0559 Mobile: 07976 236796
info@photographybytanya.co.uk
www.photographybytanya.co.uk

Sho😊t!
the Kids!

...natural photos,
in the comfort of your own **home**.

The Museum of Nottingham Life at Brewhouse Yard
Castle Boulevard, Nottingham
Tel: 0115 915 3600
Web: www.nottinghamcity.gov.uk/museums
Open daily. Experience everyday life in Nottingham over the past 300 years. Have a go at pumping water, sit in the Victorian schoolroom, root through kitchen cupboards and visit the wartime air raid shelter in the caves.

Nottingham Castle
Off Maid Marian Way, Nottingham
Tel: 0115 915 3700
Web: www.nottinghamcity.gov.uk/museums
castle@ncmg.demon.co.uk
Open daily. Cave tours of the passageways and tunnels beneath the building, tell the sites chequered history. The museum contains paintings, decorative arts, military collections and the Story of Nottingham. Plus, a children's gallery, interactive displays and a medieval playground within the grounds.

Nottingham City Museums & Galleries
NOTTINGHAM
Tel: 0115 9152731

Wollaton Hall & Park
Wollaton Park, Nottingham
Tel: 0115 915 3900
Web: www.wollatonhall.org.uk
Email: wollaton@ncmg.demon.co.uk
Open daily
Set in 500 acres, the Natural History Museum within the Hall has lots for children to do. Meet George the Gorilla, hissing cockroaches and creatures from days gone by, then venture out to the playground.

Play Houses

Castle and Cottage Playhomes
Tel: 01389 732732
Web: www.castleandcottage.com

Honeypot Playhouses
Tel: 0870 164 4002
Web: www.waltons.co.uk

Just Playhouses
Tel: 07768 727 016
Web: www.justplayhouses.co.uk

Rainbow Play
Tel: 0845 1300 335
Web: www.rainbowplay.co.uk

Portraits

Karen Harvey Portraits
48 Beech Avenue, NOTTINGHAM
Tel: 0115 9256030

Post Natal Support

The National Childcare Trust
Alexandra House, Oldham Terrace, Acton, LONDON
Tel: 0870 444 8707
Web: www.national-childbirth-trust.org.uk
The National Childbirth Trust (NCT) offers support in pregnancy, childbirth and early parenthood. There aim to give every parent the chance to make informed choices. They try to make sure that all services, activities and membership are fully accessible.

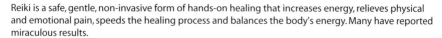

Reiki

Reiki is a safe, gentle, non-invasive form of hands-on healing that increases energy, relieves physical and emotional pain, speeds the healing process and balances the body's energy. Many have reported miraculous results.

A treatment feels like a wonderful glowing radiance that flows through you and surrounds you. Reiki is pure energy and treats the whole person including body, emotions, mind and spirit and creates many beneficial effects including deep relaxation and feelings of peace, security, and well-being.

The knowledge that an unseen energy flows through all living things and is connected directly to the quality of health has been part of the wisdom of many cultures since ancient times. The existence of this "life force energy" has been verified by recent scientific experiments, and medical doctors are considering the role it plays in the functioning of the immune system and the healing process.

An Example: The body of the mother changes immensely during and after pregnancy. Therefore, the energy-balance is constantly under pressure and is manifested emotionally and physically. The mother is more tired and unstable than normal, consequently typical pregnancy complaints arise, like, for example, morning sickness. Reiki has a positive influence on this energy-balance and when the energy is brought back in balance, these symptoms disappear.

To book a treatment, or for further details please contact Jackie on:
0115 9676792 / Mobile 07870 576293

Reflexology

Caroline Gray I.T.E.C. V.T.C.T. MGPP
44 Nottingham Road, Keyworth, NOTTINGHAM
Tel: 0115 9373784
Complementary Therapies including aromatherapy, stress massage, reflexology and hopi ear candles. Contact Caroline for an appointment.

Claire Hanson
LEICESTER
Tel: 0116 2991250

Restaurants

Altro Mondo
The Borough, Hinkley
Tel: 01455 619259

Annwell Inn & Restaurant
Anwell Lane, Smisby
Tel: 01530 413604

Antibo's Restaurant
Lower Parliament St, Nottingham
Tel: 0115 9799949

Amirul Tandori Restaurant
Leicester Road, Quorn
Tel: 01509 621362

Anmol Tandori & Balti
Woodgate, Rothley
Tel: 0116 230 1354

Antibos
Midland Road, Derby
Tel: 01332 201 700

Antibo's Restaurant
London Road, Leicester
Tel: 0116 2250000

Apurba Indian restaurant
Leicester Street, Leicester
Tel: 01664 410554

Ashmores Restaurant
Bingham Road, Ractcliffe On Trent
NOTTINGHAM
Tel: 0115 9332001

Axe & Compass
Five Ways, Hinkley
Tel: 01455 220240

Baltimore Dinner
Castle Marina, Nottingham
Tel: 0115 941 1175

Balti International
New Road, Derby
Tel: 01332 383044

Balti Nights
Vestry Road, Oakwood
Tel: 01332 832222

Balti Towers
81 Station Street, Burton On Trent
Tel: 01283 515921

Baseball Balti & Barbecue Apna Punjab
Harrington Street, Derby
Tel: 01332 771444

Bay Tree Restaurant
Potter Street, Melbourne, DERBYS
Tel: 01332 863358
Web: www.baytreerestaurant.co.uk

Bella Pasta
4-5 Angel Row, Nottingham
Tel: 0115 941 0108

Bentons Brasserie
Heathcote Street, Nottingham
Tel: 0115 959 9800

Berkeley Arms
Main Street, Wymondham
Tel: 01575 787587

Bestwood Lodge Hotel
Bestwood, Nottingham
Tel: 0115 967 0409

Bistango
St. Peters Church Yard, Derby
Tel: 01332 366660

Blenheim House
Main Street, Etwall
Tel: 01283 732254

Bluebell Inn
Farnah Green, Belper
Tel: 01773 826495

Brewer's Fayre
Hinkley Road , Leicester
Tel: 0116 239 4677

Bulls Head Inn
Main Street, Ratby
Tel: 0116 239 3256

Cafe Rouge
31 Bridlesmith Gate, NOTTINGHAM
Tel: 0115 9582230

Caffe Uno
8 Low Pavement, Nottingham
Tel: 0115 958 5780

Casa Bar and Restaurant
Arkwright Street, Trent Bridge
Tel: 0115 9852287

Capital Restaurant
Bridge Street, Uttoxeter
Tel: 01889 563600

Cartwheels Restaurant
Newark
Tel: 01636 602100

Casa
Iron Gate, Derby
Tel: 01332 341946

Cedars Bar
Main Street, Evington
Tel: 0116 271 0842

Cherry's Restaurant
De Montfort Street, Leicester
Tel: 0116 254 4773

Chopsticks
High Street, Repton
Tel: 01283 703297

Colwick Hall
Colwick, Nottingham
Tel: 0115 950 0566

Cottage Restaurant
High Street, Kegworth
Tel: 01509 672449

Dibleys Bistro
West Bridgford, Nottingham
Tel: 0115 981 9819

Dionysos Greek Restaurant
Arnold, Nottingham
Tel: 0115 926 2550

Dixie Arms
Main Street, Market Bosworth
Tel: 01455 290218

Donnington Manor
Castle Donnington, Derbys
Tel: 01332 810253

Dunes Restaurant
Barton Gate, Burton On Trent
Tel: 01283 712510

Eastern Palace Tandori
Lower High Street, Tutbury
Tel: 01283 520388

Food Mountains
Tel: 0115 9431000

Frankie & Benny's
Guild Street, Burton On Trent
Tel: 01283 546621

French Living
King Street, Nottingham
Tel: 0115 958 5885

Fresh
Goosegate, Nottingham
Tel: 0115 924 3336

George Inn
Main Street, Market Harborough
Tel: 01858 565642

Gibsons Grey Lady
Restaurant, Sharpley Hill,
Newtown Linford
Tel: 01530 243558

Golden Dragon
London Road, Shardlow
Tel: 01332 799158

Hard Rock Café
11 King Street, Nottingham
Tel: 0115 947 4201

Harry Ramsden's
Tottle Road, Nottingham
Tel: 0115 986 1304

Hoggs Bistro
Main Street, Breaston
Tel: 01332 873409

Horse & Hounds
Glen Rise, Oadby
Tel: 0116 259 2229

Ivory Café
Market Place, Uttoxeter
Tel: 01889 560224

Jade Tea Rooms
High Street, Markfield
Tel: 01530 243664

Jewel of India
Southmead Way, Derby
Tel: 01332 370701

Kam Hon Cantonese
Restaurant, Friar Gate, Derby
Tel: 01332 344828

Kilworth House Hotel
Lutterworth Road, North Kilworth
Tel: 01858 880058

King's Chinese Cuisine Restaurant
148a Mansfield Road, Nottingham
Tel: 0115 958 7209

Kings Hotel
Mount Road, Hinkley
Tel: 01455 637193

Kwei Ping Restaurant
Station Street, Burton On Trent
Tel: 01283 565193

La Gondola
Osmaston Road, Derby
Tel: 01332 332895

La Torre
Leicester Street, Melton Mowbray
Tel: 01664 500199

La Toque Restaurant
Wollaton Road, Beeston
Tel: 0115 922 2268

Lamplight Restaurant
Victoria Square, Ashbourne
Tel: 01335 342279

Lashmores Restaurant
High street, Coalville
Tel: 01530 817744

Le Mistral
Mansfield Road, Nottingham
Tel: 0115 9116116

Lion Hotel & Restaurant
Bridge Street, Belper
Tel: 01773 824033

Link Measham
High Street, Measham
Tel: 01530 272766

Loaf Restaurant
Braunstone Gate, Leicester
Tel: 0116 299 9424

Loch Fyne Restaurant
King Street, Nottingham
Tel: 0115 988 6840

Merchants Restaurant
High Pavement, Nottingham
Tel: 0115 958 9898

Morley Hayes
Main Road, Morley
Tel: 01332 780480

Mr Man's Restaurant
Wollaton Park, Nottingham
Tel: 0115 928 7788

Mrs Bridges Tea Rooms
Loseby Lane, Leicester
Tel: 0116 262 3131

New Ocean City Restaurant
Wollaton, Nottingham
Tel: 0115 928 7788

New Ocean City
Restaurant, Derby Road, Nottingham
Tel: 0115 941 0041

New Water Margin
Burton Road, Derby
Tel: 01332 290482

Newmans
Market Street, Leicester
Tel: 0116 254 2090

Nick's Restaurant
Market Place, Oakham
Tel: 01572 723199

Nosh Restaurant
Arnold, Nottingham
Tel: 0115 920 8083

Numero Due
Borough Street, Castle Donnington
Tel: 01332 814888

Observatory Restaurant & Bar
Meridien Business Park, Leicester
Tel: 0116 289 0945

Park Yacht Inn
Trent Lane, Colwick
Tel: 0115 958 4614

Pagoda Cantonese Restaurant
Greyfriar Gate, Nottingham
Tel: 0115 950 1105

Palm Court Restaurant
Duffield Road, Allestree
Tel: 01332 558107

Panda Restaurant
509 Mansfield Road, Sherwood,
NOTTINGHAM
Tel: 0115 960 7214
Cantonese restaurant offering a wide range of dishes.
Families, young children and babies welcome.

Pappa's Greek Restaurant
West Bridgford, Nottingham
Tel: 0115 9819091

Pembertons Eating Emporium Ltd
Horninglow Street, Burton On Trent
Tel: 01283 511444

Petit Paris
Kings Walk, Nottingham
Tel: 0115 947 3767

Pierre Victoire
Friar Gate, Derby
Tel: 01332 370470

Pierre Victoire
Milton Street, Nottingham
Tel: 0115 941 2850

Pizza Express
Iron Gate, Derby
Tel: 01332 349718

Pizza Express
King Street, Leicester
Tel: 0116 254 4144

Pizza Express
24-26 Goosegate, Nottingham
Tel: 0115 912 7888

Pizza Express
King Street, Nottingham
Tel: 0115 952 9095

Plough Inn
Main Street, Burton On Trent
Tel: 01283 761354

Pretty Orchid
Pepper Street, Nottingham
Tel: 0115 958 8344

Red Lion Inn
Great Bowden, Market Harborough
Tel: 01858 463106

Reynards Restaurant
Off London Road, Leicester
Tel: 0116 270 7605

Ruby Cantonese & Chinese Restaurant
Hawkins Lane, Burton On Trent
Tel: 01283 548855

Rutherfords Restaurant
Sitwell Street, Spondon
Tel: 01332 544300

Rutland Coffee House & Restaurant
High Street, Oakham
Tel: 01572 722216

Saltwater
The Cornerhouse, Nottingham
Tel: 0115 924 2664

Santa Fe
The Cornerhouse, Nottingham
Tel: 0115 853 2100

Scruffy's (Lace Market)
Stoney Street, Nottingham
Tel: 0115 911 6333

Scruffy's
Derby Road, Nottingham
Tel: 0115 947 0471

Shalimar Tandori
Midland Road, Derby
Tel: 01332 366745

Sherwood Manor
Mansfield Road, Sherwood
Tel: 0115 960 4078

Siam Corner Thai Restaurant
Osmaston Road, Derby
Tel: 01332 206220

Siam Corner Thai Restaurant
London Road, Leicester
Tel: 0116 254 4856

Staunton Stables Tea Rooms
Melbourne Road, Melbourne
Tel: 01332 864617

Talbot Hotel
Bridge Foot, Belper
Tel: 01773 822258

The Angel Inn
The Moor, Coalville
Tel: 01530 834742

The Badgers Set
Reservoir Road, Cropston
Tel: 0116 2367999

The Barn Indian Restaurant
Stubby Lane, Burton On Trent
Tel: 01283 820367

The Bell Fountain
Bell Street, Wigston
Tel: 0116 281 3856

The Black Swan
Wirksworth Road, Idrridgehay
Tel: 01773 550249

The Bridge at Gamston
Radcliffe Road, Nottingham
Tel: 0115 9813641

The Bubble Inn
Stenson Road, Stenson
Tel: 01283 703113

The Bulls Head Inn
Kelmarsh Road, Market Harborough
Tel: 01858 525637

The Caribbean Restaurant
Normanton Road, Derby
Tel: 01332 385324

The Country Park Tavern
Thorpe Hill Drive, Heanor
Tel: 01773 762856

The Crown
London Road, Leicester
Tel: 0116 259 2725

The Dial Bar & Restaurant
Station Road, Burton On Trent
Tel: 01283 544644

The George & Dragon
Ashby Road, Thringstone
Tel: 01530 222282

The Golden Crown
High Road, Beeston
Tel: 0115 9257280

The Golden Pearl
Eastwood
Tel: 01773 719 888

The Grail Curt Hotel
Station Street, Burton On Trent
Tel: 01283 732304

The Greek Restaurant
Bolebridge Street, Tamworth
Tel: 01827 316506

The Greyhound Inn
Melton Road, Burton-on-the-Wolds
Tel: 01509 880860

The Highlander
Smalley Mill Road, Horsley
Tel: 01332 780838

The Lime Kilns Inn
Watling Street, Burbage
Tel: 01455 631158

The Old Boat
Kings Bromley Road, Burton On Trent
Tel: 01283 791468

The Old Cock Inn
St Peters Road, Arnesby
Tel: 0116 247 8251

The Old Marina
London Road, Shardlow
Tel: 01332 799797

The Old Mill Wheel
Ticknall Road, Ticknall
Tel: 01283 550335

The Old Thatched Inn
Main Street, Stanton Under Bardon
Tel: 01530 242460

The Old Vicarage Restaurant
Green Lane, Derby
Tel: 01332 343933

The Old Vicarage Restaurant
Branston, Burton On Trent
Tel: 01283 533222

The Peacock
Tel: 01476 870324

The Plough Inn
Main Street, Normanton On Soar
Tel: 01509 842228

The Pump Room
Bath Street, Ashby De la Zouch
Tel: 01530 411116

The Red Lion
Grantham Road, Bottesford
Tel: 01949 842218

The Rockaway Restaurant
Station Road, Beeston
Tel: 0115 922 4570

The Rose & Crown
Main Street, Tilton on the Hill
Tel: 0116 259 7234

The Springfield Hotel
Lowdham, Notts
Tel: 0115 966 3387

The Steamboat Inn
Lock Lane, Sawley
Tel: 0115 946 3955

The Three Swans
High Street,
Market Harborough
Tel: 01858 466644

The Tollemache Arms
Main Street, Grantham
Tel: 01476 860252

The White Horse
Leicester Lane, Desford
Tel: 01455 822394

The White Post
Belper Road, Notts
Tel: 0115 930 0194

Temple Hotel & Restaurant
Temple walk, Matlock Bath
Tel: 01629 583911

TGI Friday's
The Cornerhouse, Nottingham
Tel: 0115 950 5950

Toms Brown's Restaurant
Gunthorpe, Nottingham
Tel: 0115 966 3642

Village Taverna
London Road, Derby
Tel: 01332 360850

Vision Café Bar
Parliament Street, Nottingham
Tel: 0115 912 2000

Waltons Hotel
Derby Road, Nottingham
Tel: 0115 947 5215

Watergate Restaurant
Coventry Road, Hinkley
Tel: 01455 896827

Watson's Restaurant
Upper Brown Street, Leicester
Tel: 0116 222 7770

Webster's Restaurant
Victoria Road, Draycott
Tel: 01332 874253

White House
Scraptoft Lane, Scraptoft
Tel: 0116 241 5951

Wong Kwei Cantonese
Bath Street, Ashby De LA Zouch
Tel: 01530 412394

World Service
Castle Gate, Nottingham
Tel: 0115 8475587

Yeung Sing Restaurant & Hotel
Bingham
Tel: 01949 831831

Anne Dobson-Debdale Horses
Moorhill Hallaton Road, East Norton,
LEICESTER
Tel: 01858 555795
Livery and qualified teaching yard. All ages and experience.

Barleyfields Equestrian Centre
DERBY
Tel: 01283 734798

Bassingfield Riding School
NOTTINGHAM
Tel: 0115 9816806

Beehive Pet & Pony
BURTON ON TRENT
Tel: 01283 763 981

Brooksby Equestrian Centre
LEICESTER
Tel: 01664 850850

Buckminster Lodge
LEICESTER
Tel: 01572 787544

Chestnuts Equestrian Centre
NOTTINGHAM
Tel: 01949 20151

Claybrooke Stables
LEICESTER
Tel: 01455 202511

Debdale Horses
LEICESTER
Tel: 01858 555795

Elvaston Castle Equestrian Ctr
DERBY
Tel: 01332 751927

Hardwick Lodge Stables
LEICESTER
Tel: 0116 2863056

Harringworth Manor Stables
NORTHANTS
Tel: 01572 747400

High Cross Equestrian Centre Ltd
LEICESTER
Tel: 01455 208175

Hinckley Equestrian
LEICESTER
Tel: 01455 847464
Web: www.hinckley-equestrian.co.uk

Ironstone Farm Riding School
LEICESTER
Tel: 01664 444694

Lings Lane Riding Stables
NOTTINGHAM
Tel: 0115 9372527

Markfield Equestrian Centre
LEICESTER
Tel: 01530 242373
Web: www.markfieldequestrian.co.uk

Meadow School Of Riding
LEICESTER
Tel: 01509 263782

Mere Lane Equestrian Center
LEICESTER
Tel: 0116 2710122

Moorbridge Riding Stables
DERBY
Tel: 01332 702508

Mowsley Stables
LEICESTER
Tel: 0116 2402567

Owston Lodge Equestrian Centre
LEICESTER
Tel: 01664 454520

Parkside Riding Stables
DERBY
Tel: 01773 835193

Parkview Riding School
LEICESTER
Tel: 0116 2364858

Riverside Riding Centre
LEICESTER
Tel: 01664 561233

School of National Equitation
LEICESTER
Tel: 01509 852366
Web: www.bunny-hill.co.uk

Sedgley Equestrian Ltd
LEICESTER
Tel: 01455 850305
Web: www.sedgley-equestrian.co.uk

Somerby Equestrian Centre
LEICESTER
Tel: 01664 454838
Web: www.somerbyequestrian.co.uk

South Leicestershire Riding Establishmen
LEICESTER
Tel: 01455 209407

St Clements Lodge Equestrian
NOTTINGHAM
Tel: 0115 965 2524

St Leonards Riding School
Nottingham Road, Toton,
NOTTINGHAM
Tel: 0115 9732753

The Stables
LEICESTER
Tel: 01664 840195

Thornhill Stud
LEICESTER
Tel: 01455 554206

Tissington Trekking Centre
DERBY
Tel: 01335 350276

Witham Villa Riding Centre
LEICESTER
Tel: 01455 282694
Web: www.whitamvilla.co.uk

Woodside Riding School
NOTTINGHAM
Tel: 0115 9265147

Window To The Womb
The Laurels, Russell Avenue, Wollaton,
NOTTINGHAM
Tel: 0115 8776945
Ultrasound baby bonding scan studio.

School Wear

Batties
DERBY
Tel: 01332 345659

Beezer Manufacturing Ltd
LEICESTER
Tel: 0116 261 9615

Children's Choice
17 Bridge Street, Belper, DERBYS
Tel: 01773 825865
Specialists in schoolwear. Official scout's & guide's shop, children's fashions from newborn to teens. Nursery equipment. Everything for need for your baby!

D & P Schoolwear
NOTTINGHAM
Tel: 0115 947 5128

Gohil & Co. Ltd
LEICESTER
Tel: 0116 273 4325

Inter School Logos
Chaddesden, DERBY
Tel: 01332 281311

Jackerobi
LEICESTER
Tel: 0116 267 2844

Kidzone Ltd
3 Burton Street, Melton Mowbray, LEICESTER
Tel: 01664 500100
Quality school wear & fashion from pre-school to teens.

Hamiltons
Ilkeston, DERBYS
Tel: 0115 932 6333

Morleys School Outfitters
Chilwell, NOTTM
Tel: 0115 925 8046

Morleys School Outfitters
West Bridgford, NOTTM
Tel: 0115 981 8655

Morleys School Outfitters
Arnold, NOTTM
Tel: 0115 920 4111

P & S Lee Clothing
Kimberly, NOTTM
Tel: 0115 938 5388

Pollard Gregory Ltd
Countersthorpe, LEICS
Tel: 0116 277 3854

Pupils Schoolwear
Burton-On-Trent
Tel: 01283 224512

Saint Benedict Trading Ltd
DERBY
Tel: 01332 559269

Schools - Independent

Abbotsholme School
UTTOXETER
Tel: 01889 590217
Web: www.abbotsholme.com

Arley House P.N.E.U. School
8 Station Road, East Leake,
Loughborough, LEICESTER
Tel: 01509 852229
Web: www.arley-pneu.eastleake.sch.uk
Independant school, 3-11 yrs in rural location.

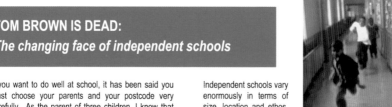

TOM BROWN IS DEAD:
The changing face of independent schools

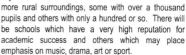

If you want to do well at school, it has been said you must choose your parents and your postcode very carefully. As the parent of three children, I know that choosing the right school for each child can be a very difficult decision. There is no such thing as the best school, but rather finding the one which will be right for the needs of your son or daughter. People today are often accused of knowing the price of everything and the value of nothing, but there is no doubt that the value of a good education is priceless.

There are over 1,200 independent schools throughout Great Britain affiliated to the Independent Schools Council, educating half a million pupils. The counties of Nottinghamshire, Leicestershire and Derbyshire are very fortunate in having a broad range of thriving and successful independent schools, educating pupils from 3-18.

> Nearly a quarter of all pupils in independent schools are given some financial help by the schools themselves and most offer various scholarships and bursaries

There is certainly no such thing as a typical independent school parent; today, they come from all occupational and social backgrounds. The majority of parents who now send their children to independent schools have not been to independent schools themselves and have no previous connection with the sector. For many parents this may involve making financial sacrifices, but they feel that they are giving something to their children which will last for the rest of their lives. With sound financial planning such an "investment for life" is possible. Some parents may choose independent schools for part of their children's education, perhaps focussing on the primary years or the sixth form.

Independent schools vary enormously in terms of size, location and ethos. There are co-educational schools and single sex schools, boarding and day schools, some in the city centre and others in more rural surroundings, some with over a thousand pupils and others with only a hundred or so. There will be schools which have a very high reputation for academic success and others which may place emphasis on music, drama, art or sport.

Most independent schools will seek a balance of all these features, whilst ensuring that they develop every child's potential to the full, in a caring and secure environment. They will offer smaller classes, high quality teaching, excellent facilities and individual attention to the needs of each child. Academic success is, of course, vital. All schools will seek to constantly challenge their pupils, both inside and outside the classroom. Michelangelo wrote that the greatest danger for most of us is not that we aim too high and fail to reach our goal, but rather that we aim too low and achieve it.

Nearly a quarter of all pupils in independent schools are given some financial help by the schools themselves and most offer various scholarships and bursaries. It is also worth remembering that many extra-curricular activities will be included as part of the extended day, which is a common feature of independent schools. Orchestra, swimming lessons and extra French will no longer require a frenzied rush for "Mum's Taxi"!

The moon-walking astronaut John Glenn said that if he lived his life again, he would choose to be a teacher rather than an astronaut, because you "touch the future". As parents, when we choose the right schools for our children, it is our opportunity to touch their future.

Robin Barlow

The Independent Schools Council information service can provide help on any aspect of independent education. The Regional Director for the Central Region, Dr Robin Barlow, offers a free telephone advisory service on 01788 570537. There is a website at www.isciscentral.info and a free handbook, listing all central region schools, can be requested by email at central@iscis.uk.net or by telephone on 01788 570537.

Ashbourne P.N.E.U. School,
ASHBOURNE
Tel: 01335 343294

Attenborough Preparatory School
NOTTINGHAM
Tel: 0115 9436725

Barlborough Hall School
DERBYS

Brooke House Day School
Croft Road, Cosby, LEICESTER
Tel: 0116 286 7576

Coteswood House School
19 Thackerays Lane, Woodthorpe,
NOTTINGHAM
Tel: 0115 9676551
Small independant school
taking children from 3-11 yrs.

Dagfa House School
57 Broadgate, Beeston, NOTTINGHAM
Tel: 0115 913 8330
Web: www.dagfahouse.notts.sch.uk

Denstone College
ROCESTER
Tel: 01889 590484

Derby Grammar
School For Boys
DERBY
Tel: 01332 523027

Derby High School
DERBY
Tel: 01332 514276

Dixie Grammar School
NUNEATON
Tel: 01455 292244

Emmanuel School
DERBY
Tel: 01332 340505

Fair Gate House School Ltd
DERBY
Tel: 01332 342765

Fairfield Preparatory School
LEICESTER
Tel: 01509 215172

Foremarke Hall
DERBY
Tel: 01283 701185
Email: office@foremarke.org.uk
Web: www.foremarke.org.uk

Gateway Christian School
DERBYS
Tel: 0115 9440609

Grace Dieu Manor School
LEICESTER
Tel: 01530 222276

Greenholme School
392 Derby Road, NOTTINGHAM
Tel: 0115 9787329
Email: enquiries@greenholme.co.uk
Web: www.greenholmeschool.co.uk
Independant co-educational day school.

Grosvenor School
NOTTINGHAM
Tel: 0115 9231184
Email: email-office@grosvenorschool.co.uk
Web: www.grosvenorschool.co.uk

Hazel Hurst Preparatory School
NOTTINGHAM
Tel: 0115 9606759

Highfield School
NOTTINGHAM
Tel: 01636 704103

Hollygirt School
Elm Avenue, NOTTINGHAM
Tel: 0115 9580596

Howitt House School
BURTON ON TRENT
Tel: 01283 820236

Iona School Association
310 Sneinton Dale, Sneinton, NOTTINGHAM
Tel: 0115 9415295

Jamia Al-Hudaa Residential College
NOTTINGHAM
Tel: 0115 9690800

Jubilee House Christian School
DERBYS
Tel: 0115 9325111

Leicester Grammar Junior School
LEICESTER
Tel: 0116 2101299

**Leicester Montessori
Preparatory School**
LEICESTER
Tel: 0116 2554445

Loughborough Endowed Schools
Burton Walks, LOUGHBOROUGH
Tel: 01509 283720

**Mansfield Prep School
& Day Nursery**
Welbeck Road,
Mansfield Woodhouse,
NOTTS
Tel: 01623 420940

**Michael House
Rudolf Steiner School**
DERBYS
Tel: 01773 718050

**Morley Hall
Preparatory School**
DERBY
Tel: 01332 674501
Fax: 1332674501

Mount St Mary's College
Spinkhill, DERBYS
Tel: 01246 433388

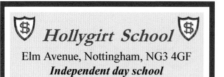

THE IONA SCHOOL
Steiner Waldorf Education

Recognizing the needs of childhood

In a rapidly changing world, it is difficult to see what political and economic conditions our children will have to face. However, we can be sure that the following are prerequisites for a healthy, positive and fulfilling life:

- emotional stability
- intellectual flexibility
- sound judgment
- inner freedom
- social awareness.

We believe that education should be a continuing process. Our task is to stimulate and develop the faculties and skills which will enable our pupils to learn:

- for life
- from life
- throughout life.

Importantly, we recognize that the child has a different consciousness from that of the adult. Children go through distinct phases of development which need to be met appropriately. During each of these phases particular faculties begin to emerge which the teacher seeks to engage in the educational process. In this way education becomes a confirming and affirming experience.

For more information about the Iona School and Nursery please contact the school office.

THE IONA SCHOOL
Steiner Waldorf Education
The school caters for children from the age of 3½ to 11/12 years. Please phone the school office to get more information. Easy access to town.

THE BEEHIVE NURSERY
Steiner Waldorf Education

The Nursery caters for children from the age of 6 weeks to 3 and a half years. We have highly qualified and experienced staff. Play focus and outdoor access daily. organic, vegetarian food - cooked on the premises daily. "For parents who value the childhood of their children"

310 Sneinton Dale,
Sneinton, NG5 7DN.
Tel: 0115 941 5295

Mount St Mary's College
Spinkhill, DERBYS
Tel: 01246 433388

Mountford House School
373 Mansfield Road, NOTTINGHAM
Tel: 0115 9605676
Email: enquiries@mountfordhouse.
nottingham.sch.uk
Web: www.mountfordhouse.
nottingham.sch.uk
*Independant co-educational
day school 3-11 years.*

Nottingham High Junior School
NOTTINGHAM
Tel: 0115 8452214
Web: www.nottinghamhigh.co.uk

Nottingham High School For Girls
NOTTINGHAM
Tel: 0115 9417663

Ockbrook School
The Settlement, Ockbrook, DERBY
Tel: 01332 673532
Web: www.ockbrook.derby.sch.uk
*The school for young achievers Ockbrook is an
independant day and boarding school on the
Notts/Derbys border.*

Our Lady's Convent School
LEICS
Tel: 01509 263901

Plumtree School
NOTTINGHAM

Ranby House School
NOTTINGHAM
Tel: 01777 703138

Ratcliffe College
Fosse Way, Ratcliffe-On-The-Wreake,
LEICESTER
Tel: 01509 817000
Email: registrar@ratcliffe.leics.sch.uk
Web: www.ratcliffecollege.com
*Independant Day & Boarding Co-educational
school. From 3-18 years.*

Repton School
DERBY
Tel: 01283 559200
Email: www.repton.org.uk

Rodney School
NOTTINGHAM
Tel: 01636 813281
Web: www.rodney-school.co.uk

Saville House School
11 Church Street, Mansfield Woodhouse,
NOTTINGHAM
Tel: 01623 625068

School House Boys Boarding
ASHBY DE LA ZCH
Tel: 01530 413759

Smallwood Manor Preparatory School
UTTOXETER
Tel: 01889 562083
Email: www.smallwoodmanor.co.uk

WELLOW HOUSE SCHOOL

Aim for the Highest
A Leading Nottinghamshire IAPS
Co-Educational,
Preparatory Day and Weekly
Boarding School

*For further details
please contact the Headmaster,*
Peter Cook,
Wellow House School, Wellow,
Newark, Notts. NG22 0EA

e-mail: wellowhouse@btinternet.com
website: www.wellowhouse.notts.sch.uk

Tel: (01623) 861054
Fax: (01623) 836665

Reg Charity no 538234

St. Crispin's School
LEICESTER
Tel: 0116 2707648
Email: saintschool@aol.com

St. Joseph's School
NOTTINGHAM
Tel: 0115 9418356
Web: www.st-josephs.nottingham.school.uk

St. Mary & St. Anne's School Abbots
BURTON ON TRENT
Tel: 01283 840232

St. Wystan's School
High Street, Repton,
DERBYSHIRE
Tel: 01283 703258
Fax: 1283703258
Email: secretary@stwystans.org.uk
Web: www.stwystans.org.uk
*Independant School and Nursery
for Boys and Girls aged between
2$^1/_2$ and 11 years old.*

GREENHOLME SCHOOL

392 Derby Road, Nottingham
*High Academic Standards
Specialist Provision for Dyslexia
Excellent Sports Facilities
Small Classes. Top Exam Results*

**INDEPENDENT
CO-EDUCATIONAL DAY SCHOOL**

Accredited by the Independent Schools
Joint Council and ISIS

**NURSERY, RECEPTION AND
PREPARATORY 3-11 +**

Prospectus available from the School Secretary
Tel: 0115 978 7329
Email: enquiries@greenholmeschool.co.uk
Website: www.greenholmeschool.co.uk

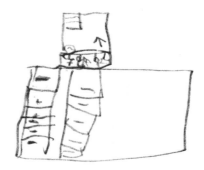

Schools
Independent

Stoneygate School
LEICESTER
Tel: 0116 2592282

The King's School
NOTTINGHAM
Tel: 0115 9539194

The Old Vicarage School
DERBY
Tel: 01332 557130

Trent College
NOTTINGHAM
Tel: 0115 8494950
Web: www.trentcollege.net

Waverley House P.N.E.U. School
13 Waverley Street, NOTTINGHAM
Tel: 0115 9783230
Independant Day School for boys and girls aged 3-11 yrs.

Wellow House School
Wellow, Newark, NOTTS
Tel: 01623 861054
Email: wellowhouse@btinternet.com
Web: www.wellowhouse.notts.sch.uk

Wolstan Preparatory School
COVENTRY
Tel: 01455 293024

Wolston Preparatory School
LEICESTER
Tel: 01455 293024

Schools - Special

Scope
6 Market Road, LONDON
Tel: 0207 7619 7100
Web: www.scope.org.uk/earlyyears
*Helpline number for finding schools is
0808 003333. Registerd Charity 208231*

Shoe Shops

Clafoutis
25 Loseby Lane, LEICESTER
Tel: 0116 2627027
*Visit Clafoutis to find good selections of popular
designer names. See main advert.*

Evolution
42 Oxford Street, Ripley, DERBYS
Tel: 01773 744553
Web: www.designerclothes4kids.co.uk
*Large selection of designer wear,
including shoes, gifts and christening wear.*

Inch Blue
CAERPHILLY
Tel: 0292 086 5863

Jellyrolls Footwear
10 St. Martins Square, LEICESTER
Tel: 0116 2425222

Junior B By Brigdens
54 Sadler Gate, DERBY
Tel: 01332 202373-384665
*Designer childrenswear including Burberry, DKNY,
Kenzo and more. Plus Christening Wear.*

Katherine Spillar
23 Mayfield Drive, NOTTINGHAM
Tel: 0115 947 0408

Kids at Scotney's
132 London Road, LEICESTER
Tel: 0116 2556942
Web: www.christopherscotney.co.uk

Little Gems
36 Bell Street, Wigston, LEICESTER
Tel: 07970 926194
*Little Gems have just moved to Wigston where
they have a selection of designer wear for babies
and children. They also stock christening wear.*

Oilily at Jellyrolls
18 Francis Street, LEICESTER
Tel: 0116 2709129

Pumpkin Patch Ltd
208-209 Victoria Centre, NOTTINGHAM
Tel: 0115 9501155

Pumpkin Patch Ltd
208-209 Victoria Centre, NOTTINGHAM
Tel: 0115 9501155

Starchild
Unit 18, Oak Business Centre
Ratcliffe Road, Sileby, LEICESTER
Tel: 01509 817601
Email: info@starchildshoes.co.uk
Web: www.starchildshoes.co.uk
*Soft leather baby shoes, handmade in England.
Practical and fun.*

Skating Rinks

Rollerworld
Mansfield Road, DERBY
Tel: 01332 345828

National Ice Centre
Belero Square, The Lace Market, NOTTINGHAM
Tel: 0115 853 3000

Ski Slopes

The Snowdome
TAMWORTH
Tel: 08705 000011

The Play Centre
NOTTINGHAM
Tel: 0115 9693432

Support Groups

Parentline Plus
61B Mansfield Road, NOTTINGHAM
Tel: 0115 9500036
Email: contact@parentlineplus.org.uk
Web: www.parentlineplus.org.uk
*Support for parents, freephone helpline courses
and workshops, leaflets etc.*

Swimming Lessons

A & K Swimming School
NOTTINGHAM
Tel: 0115 9174561
*Private swimming lessons from 4 upwards at the
Nottingham High School. Toddler groups held and
Hydrotherapy pool at Long Eaton. For further
information contact Amanda 0115 9174561.*

Maternity Tens Hire
Covering Derbys, Leicesters & Notts
Tel: 01332 812825
Email: sales@maternitytens.com
Drug free pain relief. Safe for Mother & baby. Next day delivery service. For sale or hire from £20.00. Tens machines are battery operated devices that emit small pulses that block the pain signal being sent from the brain, whilst stimulating the natural release of endorphins

Tour Operators

Cathay Pacific
Tel: 0208 834 8888
Web: www.cathypacific.com

Club Med
Tel: 0845 367 6767
Web: www.clubmed.co.uk
44 Villages worldwide with liddy clubs (seven with baby clubs from four months).

Crystal Holidays
Tel: 01235 824324
Web: www.crystalholidays.co.uk
Sking & summer holidays. Nannny-share schemes.

Japan Airlines
Tel: 0845 774 7700
Web: www.jal-europe.com

KLM
Tel: 0870 507 4074
Web: www.klm.com

Mark Warner
Tel: 0870 770 4222
Web: www.markwarner.co.uk
One of the best-known children freindly tour operators, with beach resorts and chalet hotels in Europe. Chilcare and nanny service available for babies from four months.

Powder Bryne
Tel: 0208 246 5300
Web: wwww.powderbyrne.com
Worldwide resorts plus ski holidays. Creches a childrens activity clubs.

Tourist Attractions

Rainbow Tours
Tel: 0207 226 1004
Web: www.rainbowtours.co.uk
Tailor made family holiday to some of the best destinations.

Ski Esprit
Tel: 01252 618300
Web: www.espirit-holidays.co.uk
These are specialist in family skiing holidays, mainly in France.

The Adventure Company
Tel: 01420 541007
Web: www.adventurecompany.com
Great Family holidays worldwide.

Attenborough Nature Centre
NOTTINGHAM
Tel: 0115 9721777
Web: www.attenboroughnaturecentre.co.uk

Rushcliffe Country Park
Set in the beautiful South Nottinghamshire Countryside open for you to enjoy throughout the year.

Facilities & Features:-

- Environmental Education Centre available for hire for schools, community groups & business.
- 210 acres of Country Park
- Lake & wildlife habitats
- 5 miles of wheelchair/pushchair accessible footpaths
- Children's play area & skate ramp
- Picnic Areas
- Seasonal catering facilities
- Toilets & baby changing facility

Why not visit Nottingham Transport & Heritage Centre (open sundays seasonally) 0115 9405705

Contact the Head Ranger; Rushcliffe Country Park, Mere Way Ruddington, Nottingham, NG11 6JS. Tel: **0115 9215865** Rushcliffe

Belvoir Castle
Belvoir, LEICS
Tel: 01476 871002

Bestwood Country Park
NOTTINGHAM
Tel: 0115 9273674

City of Caves
NOTTINGHAM
Tel: 0115 9881955

Naturescape
LANGAR
Tel: 01949 860592
Email: sales@naturescape.co.uk
Web: www.naturescape.co.uk

Nottingham Transport Heritage Centre
NOTTINGHAM
Tel: 0115 940 5705
Email: mailbox.nthc.co.uk
Web: www.nthc.co.uk

Rushcliffe Country Park
Mere Way, Ruddington, NOTTINGHAM
Tel: 0115 9215865
210 acres of beautiful young parkland & conservation areas. Childrens play area.

Sherwood Forest Farm Park
Lamb Pen Farm Park, Edwinstowe,
NR MANSFIELD, Notts
Tel: 01623 823558
Web: www.sherwoodforestfarmpark.co.uk
Great day out for parents and children.

The National Space Centre
Exploration Drive, LEICESTER
Tel: 0870 6077223

The Tales of Robin Hood
NOTTINGHAM
Tel: 0115 9501536

Watermead Country Park
LEICESTER
Tel: 0116 2671944

White Post Farm Centre
Mansfield Road, Farnsfield, NOTTS
Tel: 01623 882977
Email: www.whitepostfarmcentre.co.uk
Great day out for all the family. Make friends with over 3,000 animals. Suitable for children 1-100!

Tourist Information Centres

Wickstead Park
Barton Road, Kettering, NORTHANTS
Tel: 01536 512475

Wonderland
Whitepost, Farnsfield, NOTTS
Tel: 01623 882773
Simply more to see and do!

Rutland Water Tourist Information
Sykes Lane, Empingham
Tel: 01572 653026

Tourist Information Centre
Flore's House, 34 High Street
Tel: 01572 724329

Tourist Information Centre
Town Hall, Loughborough, LEICS
Tel: 01509 218113

Tourist Information Centres
The Gilstrap Centre, Castle Gate,Newark, NOTTS
Tel: 01636 655765

Tourist Information Centres
County Hall, West Bridgford NOTTINGHAM
Tel: 0115 9773358

Toy Shops

A Bear's Life
NOTTINGHAM
Tel: 0115 9423366

Arbon & Watts Ltd
LEICESTER
Tel: 01664 850010

Arcade Neanies & Collectables
NOTTINGHAM
Tel: 0115 9550545

Bear & Bits
DERBY
Tel: 01332 203620

Bear Factory
NOTTINGHAM
Tel: 0115 9242739

Beecrofts Toys Ltd
NOTTINGHAM
Tel: 01522 778885

Brownz Toyz
LEICESTER
Tel: 01455 233949

Curtis Brae of Stratford
LEICESTER
Tel: 01789 267277
Web: www.curtisbrae.co.uk

Dolls House Cottage Workshop
NOTTINGHAM
Tel: 0115 9465059

Dominoes
LEICESTER
Tel: 0800 5423071

Early Learning Centre
LEICESTER
Tel: 0116 2625092

Early Learning Centre
NOTTINGHAM
Tel: 0115 9474203

Geoff's Toys
LEICESTER
Tel: 01509 216966

Highwaymen Kites Ltd
LEICESTER
Tel: 01455 230736

Hill Ridware Activity Toys
RUGELY
Tel: 01543 491667

Kid's World UK
LEICESTER
Tel: 01530 814037
Web: www.kidsworlduk.com

Nik Nak Toys
The Lodge, Eastend,
Damerham, HAMPSHIRE
Tel: 0845 644 7025
Web: www.niknaktoys.co.uk
Imaginative fun and affordable wood and soft toys for children. Buy on line, mail order or catalogue.

Rob-Roy Wooden Toy
81 College Street, Long Eaton, NOTTINGHAM
Tel: 0115 9733943

Shellbrook Toys
LEICESTER
Tel: 01530 412185

Slawston Swings & Slides
LEICESTER
Tel: 01858 555450

Solutions
LEICESTER
Tel: 01858 462208

Teddy Bear UK
NOTTINGHAM
Tel: 0115 9812013
Web: www.teddy-bears-uk.com

The Entertainer
NOTTINGHAM
Tel: 0115 9241325

Towns Cottage Toys
LEICESTER
Tel: 01858 575397

Toy Box
Unit 4 Bull Yard, King Street,
Southwell, NOTTINGHAM
Tel: 01636 816869

Toymaster
LEICESTER
Tel: 01530 832795

Toy Shops

Toymaster
DERBY
Tel: 01332 366336

Toymaster at Thorpes
DERBYS
Tel: 0115 9327834

Toys 'R' Us Ltd
NOTTINGHAM
Tel: 0115 9851185

Toys 'R' Us Ltd
BERKS
Tel: 01628 414141

Tyler Ltd
NOTTINGHAM
Tel: 01825 891900
Web: www.pedalkarts.co.uk

Wicken Toys Ltd
MILTON KEYNES
Tel: 01908 571233
Web: www.wickentoys.co.uk

Wood & Toys
NOTTINGHAM
Tel: 01636 613131

Wooden Tots Luxury Toys
NOTTINGHAM
Tel: 0800 5873597
Web: www.woodentotsluxurytoys.co.uk

Woolgars Toys
LEICESTER
Tel: 01455 558848
Web: www.woolgars.co.uk

www.cafamily.org.uk
A directory with details of medical conditions and medical support groups

www.disabilty.gov.uk
Gives more information of the Disability Discrimination Act (1995)

www.mencap.org.uk
Gives you the national picture, range of services through organisation for people with a learning disability. It also gives local contacts.

www.rnib.gov.org
Gives information on the society for the blind.

www.ace-ed.org.uk
The advisory centre for Education's web site

www.bda-dyslexia.org.uk
Detailed Information for Dyslexia

www.oneworld/autism-uk
The official site for the Autistic Society

www.scope.org.uk
Gives more information for people with Cerebral Palsy

www.croner.cch.co.uk
This site is a catalogue of resources available on-line.

W

Active Birth Centre
Tel: 020 7281 6760
Web: www.activebirthcentre.com

Splashdown Water Births Services
Park Farm, 81 Town Green Street, ROTHLEY
Tel: 0870 444 4403

Working Opportunites

Body Shop Parties
8 Walton Road, Chaddesdon,
DERBYS
Tel: 01332 735564

La Jolie Ronde
43 Long Acre, Bingham, NOTTS
Tel: 01949 839715

"Know Your Mind, Love Your Body"

*Part-time/Full Time Consultants required.
Hours to suit. Write your own pay cheque.
Excellent Career Plan.*

Ring Annie Beddows,
Area Manager
01332 735564/07958 754132
annie.b1@ntlworld.com
*Or call to book a party for a
fun night in with friends.*

THE BODY SHOP at Home

"Bonjour,
I speak fluent French and run my own business teaching Primary school children with the famous La Jolie Ronde method.
Mairi, Notts

It's great because La Jolie Ronde continually supports me with training, marketing and proven quality course material. It's also very rewarding and satisfying belonging to the UK's leading Primary French language organisation.
Join me and the 400 plus licensed centres - you'll really enjoy the experience!"
There are opportunities to grow with La Jolie Ronde throughout the UK.
Call now on 01949 839715, e.mail us at info@lajolieronde.co.uk or apply on line at www.lajolieronde.co.uk
Please quote reference LJR1104 4

Yoga & Yoga for Kids

Claire Hanson
LEICESTER
Tel: 0116 2991250

The Yoga Place
Unit D18, Hartley Business Centre,
Haydn Road, Sherwood, NOTTINGHAM
Tel: 0115 9691233
Web: www.theyogaplace.co.uk
A place dedicated to the practice & development of yoga excellence.

Happy Kids Yoga
NOTTINGHAM
Tel: 0115 9676792
Email: happykidsyoga@ntlworld.com

Yoga Bugs
20 Needham Road, Arnold, NOTTINGHAM
Tel: 0115 9676792

Zoos

See Tourist Attractions

162

Stretching Imagination

A big problem recently reported is that in the UK almost one in 12 six-year-olds can now be classed as obese, according to the Health Development Agency.

Children today do spend far too much time sitting down playing computer games or watching television rather than engaging in physical activity. Coupled with too much fatty junk food is a recipe for disaster.

This is where YogaBugs comes to the rescue. In our classes we learn the importance of looking after our body to keep it strong and healthy. We learn the significance of our breathing and how it can help to achieve calmness and how to relax achieving a clearer mind that is able concentrate at a much higher level. We raise self-esteem and confidence through constant praise along with affirmations, all wonderful tools greatly needed in children's lives today.

Yoga can help children suffering from stress close to their SATS tests. We teach children how to relax

and clear their minds in order for them to be able to focus and concentrate much easier with the task in hand. A Yoga class on the day of their tests will help calm them down and may even be able to help with those important results!

The benefits are clear for youngsters of all ages and ability, and great results can be seen in those suffering with poor concentration, autism, respiratory problems such as asthma, migraines and sleeping difficulties to name a few.

A YogaBugs class is a haven for kids to be imaginative, creative and to have fun.

Our classes are designed in the form of wonderful fun games and fantastic adventures to many different places to make it a fun way exercising.

Weekly classes help to improve balance, co-ordination and confidence as well as encouraging relaxation. Children will inevitably have a healthier body, better focus and improved concentration, which will be invaluable to them for many years to come.

Do you enjoy reading autobiographies and social histories?

Then this book is for you!

Valerie the Whirlwind tells of her family background and of her mother working at Bletchley Park during the war, of Bletchley in the 1960s and her nurse training at the world famous Stoke Mandeville Hospital.

Working in the Mental Health field, she provides tales of experiences, as a Community Psychiatric Nurse for 26years, of interesting patients and difficult situations.

It tells of the many adventures volunteering in St John Ambulance and later, when free of family commitments, she is able to become a volunteer nurse abroad in Jerusalem, Cape Town and Malaysia.

Spending six months and many other visits to Jerusalem, Valerie is able to give an insight into places away from the tourist sites, with the proceeds of the books going to the St John Eye Hospital Jerusalem.

I hope that you can support my venture & enjoy the read.

Would anyone at Church buy a copy?

Please encourage your relatives, friends and associates to purchase this book, as the proceeds are for the St John Eye Hospital Jerusalem, a charity dear to my heart.

Please order from:
Mrs Valerie Young OstJ
23 Smugglers Wood Road
Christchurch
Dorset BH23 4PJ   Tel: 01425-501005
Mob: 07958680718   Email: theyoungteam2001@hotmail.com

Colour copies: £22   Black and White copies: £12
Please add £3 for postage and packing.

Cheques made payable to Valerie Young
For BACS payment:

Sort code 40-47-84   Account no 91849956   Mrs Valerie Margaret Young

_____

Please send me _____ copies of Valerie The Whirlwind

I enclose £_____ for _____ copies and cheque for £_____

Name:

Address: Telephone number:

Post code: Email:

Valerie: The Whirlwind

My Life & Adventures

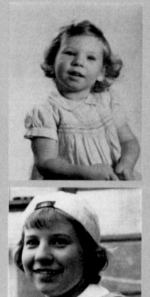

Valerie Young